LETTERS FROM
TINIAN 1945

LETTERS FROM TINIAN 1945

Enjoy —

Pauline Denman Webb

❖

Pauline D. Webb,
(Lt. Pauline A. Denman,
A. N. C. WWII)

Library of Congress Control Number: 2009906359
ISBN: Hardcover   978-1-4415-4927-3
                 Softcover   978-1-4415-4926-6

This book was printed in the United States of America.

To order additional copies of this book, contact:
Xlibris Corporation
1-888-795-4274
www.Xlibris.com
Orders@Xlibris.com
64476

DEDICATION

I dedicate this book to my children, Debra and John, who
have been the greatest joy of my life

ACKNOWLEDGMENTS

I would like to thank my family and my friends for their patience in waiting for "my manuscript" to come to fruition, (following over ten years of promises). My greatest gratitude goes to my daughter Debra, who dragged me kicking and screaming into the computer world by bringing me a computer, (throwing out my Royal portable), and teaching me how to use "the thing" . . . Frustration for me and great patience on her part. Also thanks to my friend Cynthia Lauten for reviewing "Letters from Tinian 1945" in manuscript form. Her editing and suggestions have been most helpful.

For accuracy of historical events I perused many books, encyclopedias, newspaper articles, my personal World War II scrapbook, etc

A few books of interest:

"Mission Hiroshima" by Paul W. Tibbets, Commander of the Enola Gay

"War's End" by Maj. Gen Charles W. Sweeney, U.S.A.F. (Ret.)

"Enola Gay" by Gordon Thomas and Max Morgan Witts

"Day One" by Peter Wyden

INTRODUCTION

The nuclei of this manuscript is the letters from an attic of my parents, letters written by me as an army nurse in 1945 from Tinian Island in the western Pacific, near the end of the war and during the occupation of Japan.

To that extent this is a memoir, as the letters are printed just as written with the only exception being the change of names where prudent. The pseudonyms are used as it would be inappropriate in an historical memoir to do any editing of information that might seem unimportant, uninteresting or too personal as in the case of a diary.

The rest of the story is primarily true but with a bit of fiction.

PROLOGUE

18 October 1945
Last night on Tinian

It was pitch black, dark as a pocket, and quiet. It was like being alone, but I wasn't. There were several dozen other nurses in our quonset on an island in the Pacific. Were they all lying awake wondering as I was—what next?

It must be after midnight, it seems like hours since "Lights Out" at 2200 (10 PM) Unable to sleep, I've been lying here wondering and maybe worried a bit about tomorrow. The war has been over for a couple of months so no worry about that. We ship out, but we don't know where, though latrine rumor has it we will go to Japan.

Tossing and turning my mind wanders to other departures and my thoughts at that time. It was different then, with nothing but adventures ahead. While at my first station assignment at Ft Monmouth, NJ, a notice appeared on the bulletin board for nurses to sign up and volunteer for duty overseas. I signed up with some second thoughts as had occurred when I mailed in my application to join the army shortly after passing my state boards and receiving my RN.

My assignment there at Ft. Monmoth had been night duty (1800-0600,. 6 PM to 6 AM) in Obstetrics for 31 nights, no time off. Obstetrics wasn't exactly my idea of army duty, but I enjoyed the work as always with new babies and their families. Next came a month in ortho-pedics where they couldn't polish the floors for obvious reasons. Making it a hardship to be all "Spit and polish" for the monthly inspection, in competition with the other wards. But we tried other tactics by putting all the patients stuff on a stretcher and shoving it in the linen closet out of sight. Good thing the colonel didn't inspect the linen closet.

The linen closet was used for other things, like sneaking in there with my ward master Floyd Smith for a hug and kiss. Being an officer I wasn't supposed to fraternize with Floyd, but we really liked each other and would have to sneak off the base separately for an evening out of dancing.

I was pretty excited when the orders came for shipment to Camp Kilmer, NJ, to await a ship for overseas duty in the E.T.O. (European Theater of Operations). I knew I would miss Floyd, but I was eager for our next move.

PAULINE D. WEBB, (LT. PAULINE A. DENMAN, A. N. C. WWII)

While at Kilmer we went dancing at the officer's club nightly (it was called "The Bloody Bucket"), and didn't do any nursing assignments, just waited for orders. We never made it to The E. T. O. While awaiting our shipping orders, President Roosevelt died and the war ended in Europe. What next? No anxiety, just curious about our next assignment.

Orders finally came through. It was time to pack and board a train in the middle of the night, no hint to where we were going, but we soon arrived at Fort Bragg, NC, into a hot climate with nothing but winter issue clothing to wear. They soon had us ship our winter issue clothing back home and get some summer issue clothing. Next stop, the Pacific.

We joined the rest of the personnel for a unit called the 308 General Hospital, and had classes every day about mosquitoes, malaria, etc. etc. Also working full time. Nights again! Are they trying to hide me in the dark? I was supervisor of five wards, black soldiers who were pretty entertaining at times. One lad wanted me to write a letter to his girl back home (he had a broken arm) and "make it mushy". I did my best. Another would walk down the hall with me, limping on the wrong foot. I would remind him of it. He was trying to get out of the service on a Section Eight discharge (mental).

Again I was on twelve hour nights for one full month (no days off), and struggling to sleep in the noisy barracks. Mildred, another nite nurse and I finally decided to sleep in the woods. Not only was the ground hard and bumpy, we learned about Chiggers! They crawled under tight clothing, bit and burrowed under the skin. And did it itch! No remedy really worked, i.e. burning end of a cigarette, ether, etc. The only cure was the " tincture of time". We survived but never slept outside again. Never had that problem in basic training in AtlanticCity, NJ on bivouac.

We did have time for a little fun now and then. We dated fliers from nearby Pope Field and played a lot of Bridge. One day a group of us all piled in a car, some of us in the trunk and headed for a beach on a lake in South Carolina. One doctor always had a cigar in his mouth, whether he was on the shore or in the water. It was a good diversion. But mostly we had classes and duty on the wards until orders finally came and we boarded a train to where? You never know in the army. You just follow orders and go. No regrets on leaving some of my dates, Fran's brother and Jack Cassell. They were just friends.

We headed by train again, west thru Chattanooga, Tenn., thence to Washington state. I really enjoyed the scenery of our West, places I had never been. We ended up in Fort Lewis, near Seattle, a point of embarkation for the Pacific theater. There was a war going on and we were on our way.

All my thoughts of past times and departures must have put me to sleep because it was now morning and the others were beginning to stir. Our footlockers had gone to the port yesterday and all we had to do was get dressed, stuff the rest of our odds and ends into our barrack bags and head for the door.

PART ONE

THE JOURNEY

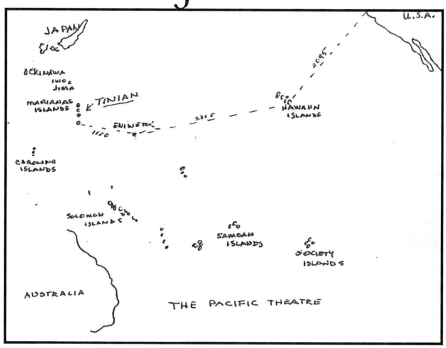

The Pacific Theatre

THE PRESENT

It was a lovely June morning, "What is so rare . . . ?" The dishes were done. Sam had gone to pick up his son for the day and Deb and I were relaxing on the deck just outside the kitchen door

This is how Sundays had been enjoyed. almost every Sunday since my daughter Deb met Sam several years ago and soon were married. The three of us would have Sunday brunch at my house and enjoy all kinds of discussions over coffee. We'd discuss everything from family activities to world affairs all the way down to how to build a " better cat litter box".

This morning Deb was sitting there tatting and I was doing the Sunday crossword puzzle outside in the lovely fresh air. We hadn't yet decided how to spend the rest of the day.

Deb chanced to ask if I still had those old letters from Mom and Dad's attic, letters I had written home from overseas when I was in the Army Nurse Corps in World War II.

I hadn't given much thought to those army days for a long time. I couldn't remember what I had done with the letters. We had moved several times. I vaguely remembered cleaning out an old footlocker when we sold our home in Pompano Beach, FL and moved to a townhouse in Coconut Creek, FL. I threw a lot of things away including the footlocker.

Eight years later I moved to Jacksonville, FL to be near my daughter where she had purchased a home while performing with a professional ballet company. But I did remember a box of family memorabilia up on a closet shelf in my den.

The sun was moving around onto the deck and it was time to move inside, so I went into the den in search of the letters. After a short time I found them tucked down in the box of many unrelated items I had kept from the past.

The letters were in two packs tied with ribbons and in order by date beginning in July 1945 in the middle of the Pacific aboard a ship. I started reading them aloud to Deb. It was almost like reading the letters of a stranger. It had been so long since I had written them that they were almost unfamiliar to me. It had been well over fifty years since I had written the letters. I had lived several lifetimes since then,—been married and widowed twice, had two children and two grandchildren.

PAULINE D. WEBB, (LT. PAULINE A. DENMAN, A. N. C. WWII)

I read the letters aloud until I was hoarse. Deb was so fascinated, she finished reading the rest to herself. Just reading the ones that I did, transported me back to that small window of time. You never really forget things as important as love and war.

Deb was so serious after reading all of the letters that she immediately uncovered my copying machine and proceeded to make copies of all the letters to have at her house in case anything happened to the originals here. She said I should get them published, not just for their historical significance, but because they showed the contrast between the tedium of day to day things one does even though in the middle of a war arena, and the enormity of what is actually happening in the war.

Her interest and suggestion are the reasons why I have assembled this manuscript.

17 JULY 1945

On this date the U. S. S. Matsonia shipped out of Seattle, Washington State. with the female personnel of the 308th General Hospital on board among thousands of other service people.

Also on this date was the opening of the Potsdam Conference. Churchill, Stalin and Truman discuss the problems of peace in Europe and the conditions for the solution of the war against Japan.

Aircraft took off from ships of the U. S. Fleet and the British Pacific Fleet began a series of bombardment of military installations and airfields in the Tokyo area.

SOMEWHERE IN THE PACIFIC 1945

This letter was written aboard the U. S. S. Matsonia a Matson Line cruise ship turned over for use in transporting personnel, etc., to war zones. It had been re-equipped for that use. For example, the swimming pool had been drained and served as quarters for troops being sent overseas.

LETTERS FROM TINIAN 1945

AFTER SEVERAL DAYS AT SEA
STILL AT SEA AS ALWAYS JULY 1945 ON USS MATSONIA

Dearest Mom and Dad,

The letter I wrote the other day is still here beside me. I haven't noticed us passing any post offices lately but someday maybe one will come along.

I haven't yet had a report on your trip to Vermont and Massachusetts. The only report I've had from you since your vacation was a post card from dad asking how I liked California, assuming I had been there as my APO was San Francisco. Some day I should get a pile of mail. What a blessing that will be.

I presume by now that Midge and Dave are vacationing. As far as that goes, I'm having quite a vacation myself—and getting paid for it too. Never thought I'd be going on an ocean voyage, with all expenses paid.

I've been eating like a horse and getting fresh air and now and then some sunshine. Not too much of the latter because my skin couldn't take it.

Remember the trips we used to take on the Hudson? This is just like it except the boat rocks a little more. I'm amazed that I have had no nausea at all but a lot of the girls have. Peterson lost both of her suppers the other night. I guess I live right. Everyone is getting used to it now. I just roll from side to side in my bunk and think nothing of it. I walk along the hall and get thrown from the port bulkhead to the starboard and sometimes the deck comes up to meet my feet. All I have to show for it is one skinned knee and one black and blue knee. It's really wonderful though.

The ocean is simply gorgeous. It is a different color every now and then. Sometimes it's angry and with white caps while other times it is very calm.

This is the last sheet of this kind of paper so I will have to cut it short.

Last night Jim and I went to a screwy movie on board, "Murder He Says" starring Fred MacMurray. It was really corney but I smiled all the while while everyone else split their sides laughing. I think you'd enjoy it.

I guess I'll write to Midge and Dave now. You, Net and O'Bean and Cookie are the only ones I've written to as yet.

I'm having a wonderful time. Wish you could share it with me sometime.

Love and kisses,

"Pill"

PILL

Since the majority of my letters are signed "Pill", I should elucidate about the use of that name. It was an early childhood nickname. I suppose "Pauline " was too cumbersome so it progressed from Pauline to "Paul" to "Pill", never " Polly" or Addie, my middle name. Just plain Pill.

After the war and when I moved away from my hometown I seldom used that nickname. Many years later when my children were in grade school and we lived in Rhode Island, a knock came on the door. I opened it to find Jim Holmes standing there. He was an old friend from Slingerlands, NY who smiled and said, "Hi Pill". That's all it took. Deb was right there and heard me called "Pill". She grabbed it and ran with it and has called me Pill ever since. We always called Jim, "Betty Crocker" as he worked for General Mills

My sister's name was Marjorie but she was always called, "Midge". I have no idea why, except it did seem to suit her. It seems nicknames just seem to evolve

According to the dictionary, a pill is:

1. A small globular or rounded mass of medicinal substance to be swallowed whole.
2. Something unpleasant that has to be accepted or endured.
3. Slang, a disagreeable or unpleasant person, etc.

But when it starts with a capitol "P" it is yours truly.

JULY 1945

President Truman was in Potsdam, Germany in conference when he heard the details of the successful test of the first atom bomb at Alamagordo, New Mexico on 6 July. In the summer of 1941, intensive research and development had begun in earnest preceding this test. Major General Leslie Groves was the director of this effort, code named "Manhattan Project" a super secret activity. So secret that I never knew until many, many years later that my sister and her husband had worked with General Groves on that project.

*   *   *

The USS Indianapolis sailed to the Pacific Island of Tinian to deliver vital parts of the atom bomb. The trip with its very secret, heavily guarded cargo made it safely from San Francisco to Tinian. The cargo was a cup shaped chunk of Uranium 235, the main fissile component of "Little Boy" the atomic bomb destined for Hiroshima.

The USS Indianapolis was struck by Japanese torpedoes after departing Tinian, and sunk. Eight hundred crewmen lost their lives. Three hundred sixteen people survived after five days afloat in shark infested waters, suffering from salt water poisoning and dehydration.

An Army Air Corps patrol discovered them by accident.

TINIAN ISLAND

Tinian Island is located in the western Pacific Ocean, one of the Mariana Islands, part of a chain of islands formed by the summits of a submerged mountain range that extends from Saipan almost to Japan. It is about 1500 miles southeast of Tokyo covering an area of about thirty nine square miles, about the size and shape of Manhattan. It was captured from Japan by the Marines in July 1944.

Tinian and two other Mariana islands, Guam and Saipan were used as air bases for B-29s during WWII because they were within air range of Japan. On Tinian was constructed the biggest operational airport in the world where fleets of B-29s conducted almost daily raids against Japan.

When U. S. Forces occupied Tinian during the war, they laid out a system of roads with the same general plan and orientation as on the island of Manhattan back home with Broadway being the main north-south road. From the time the Marines took the island in July 1944 to the end of the war, many, many months of labor and ingenuity went into making Tinian the most talked about island in the Pacific and the "Fear All" arsenal of the entire world.

It was the great work of the Seebees that created a Tinian Base for the needs of the Army Air Force.

Mt. Lasso was the highest point on Tinian at 564 feet. The terrain was low rises and plains. The foliage on the island was sugar cane fields on the flat areas and scrubby brush and jungle on the slopes of the higher ground.

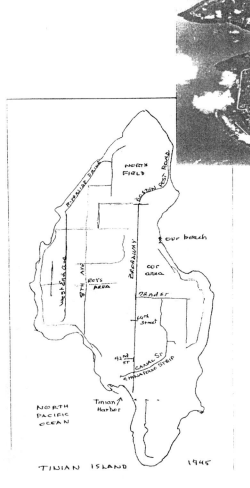

TINIAN ISLAND 1945
North Field in foreground

NORTH
FIELD

RIVERSIDE DRIVE

BOSTON POST ROAD

our beach

our area

BROADWAY

8TH AVE

Ross AREA

WEST END AVE

72nd St

64th Street

42nd ST

CANAL ST

SIMULATION STRIP

Tinian Harbor

NORTH
PACIFIC
OCEAN

TINIAN ISLAND   1945

The 'Enola Gay' - a B29 Superfortress

Lt. Denman

509TH COMPOSITE GROUP

On those small thirty-nine square miles called Tinian Island were stationed 40,000 service personnel. None of those on the southern part of the island knew what was occurring at the highly secret North Field area, only that it was off limits with top secret security.

Ironically, Tinian was known as, "Manhattan in the Pacific" because of it's shape and comparable size (and with the streets laid out in similar configuration), but as it turned out, it was at that very secure North Field area (509th Composite Group) that the results of the "Manhattan Project" were being implemented. The Enola Gay was there.

WENDOVER FIELD
UTAH 1944

A special unit of the Army Air Force was assembled here in late 1944, called the 509th Composite Group under Col. Paul W. Tibbets, Jr.. He was selected for his outstanding service and abilities. The single tactical squadron of the Bombardment 509th, the 393rd Squadron was commanded by Major Charles W. Sweeney. The. establishment of this group was by direction of the War Department and the Second Air Force. This location was chosen for its isolation, required by the secrecy of the 509th mission.

The existence of the 509th Group was not released until after the war. Their training was TOP SECRET. The 509th was the first USAAF bombardment group to be organized, equipped and trained for atomic warfare.

While at Wendover this group immediately began training in specially modified B-29 Superfortress bombers. At that time the B-29 was the largest long range bomber in the U.S. arsenal.

In early 1945, the 509th conducted intensive training in the operation and maintenance of the B-29s. To that end a search was made in the Air Force for technicians able to handle the special modifications and other requirements. About 80% of the men selected were eventually rejected. The exacting requirements and selection criteria for this priority mission were for men with skills such as welding, machinist talent and brought in from the Air Corps and ground forces.

In addition to the training and maintenance of the B-29, the 509th trained for the conduct of radar bombing missions from 20,000 to 30,000 feet, both at Wendover and other bases. After training was completed in April 1945 the main ground echelon left Wendover by plane and ship , arriving at Tinian Island on 29 May 1945. The aircraft flew to Tinian, arriving after stopovers at other bases during the last two weeks of May 1945. By mid June 1945 most of the 509th were at their base on Tinian. However, throughout July and August, specialty groups, individuals and equipment continued to arrive. They took over eighty-nine quonset huts, a mess hall, and other buildings , operating from North Field, Tinian Island. At it's peak the 509th had a total o f 225 officers and 1542 enlisted men.

LETTERS FROM TINIAN 1945

TINIAN ISLAND
SUMMER 1945

Dearest Mom and Dad:

Arrived safely, establishing a beach head under the blaze of flash bulbs and newsreel cameramen. No kidding. Maybe I'll be in a newsreel one of these days.

Happy Birthday Mom. This may even arrive before your birthday.

Don't know if Tinian is on your map but it is near to Guam and in sight of Saipan. (Excuse spelling.) This island doesn't appear very tropical, with the exception of a few banana trees (without bananas) it looks an awful lot like New York dairy land. Wouldn't mind seeing a few cows, but they are a thing to be forgotten for the present anyway.

An outdoor movie theater is just across the street and I can hear the music as I lie here on my bed.

You should see our latrine. An eight seater privy outside with a tent around it. We are slowly but surely losing our modesty.

I have a window by my bed and a nice cool breeze is blowing in. The climate here seems nice except for frequent sudden showers. On ship our compartments were way down low so our port holes were locked shut so we had no breeze. Most everyone slept on the sundeck to keep cool but I never tried it 'cause it was too hard. I put my mattress on the floor of my compartment and directed the electric fan on me. Even then I often woke up with my body sopping wet with sweat. I usually spent the day in my compartment in my bathing suit. The sun on the water was too bright for my skin.

It gets dark here shortly after supper which seems very queer for this time of the year. I have no idea what day or what hour it is at home.

My radio is here beside me all in one piece. I haven't plugged it up yet to see if it works. I'm keeping my fingers crossed.

I have written to JJ Lampson. He might even end up here for all we know. I don't think Jack Cassell is here.

Received a nice letter from Alta. Nothing else new at present. What a messy letter.

Gotta hit the sack now and sleep away a few hours.

All my love and don't worry. I'm having a wonderful time and am well, not even a sniffle. Here's hoping you are the same.

Love,

Pill

QUONSET HUT

Our living quarters were Quonset huts.

The Quonset hut was created to satisfy the need for a building to house people and supplies during the war. The need was for it to be cheap, light weight, portable and able to be constructed by untrained people.

A production facility was set up near Quonset, Rhode Island and production was begun immediately. They were constructed of rows of semicircular steel ribs covered with corrugated sheet metal. The steel foundation had a plywood floor. The larger model was 40 by 100 feet, the basic model being 48 feet long and 20 feet wide, with 720 feet of usable floor space

Our hut was one large dormitory-like room where we slept on cots. There were two small rooms near the front entry, one being the office. Our entry was in the end of the building whereas some Quonsets had a side entry.

PAULINE D. WEBB, (LT. PAULINE A. DENMAN, A. N. C. WWII)

INSIGHT INTO THE ACTIVITIES AT THE "OFF LIMITS" AREA
NORTH FIELD, TINIAN ISLAND 1945

Formerly occupied by the Seebees, the area of the 509th was located at the corner 125th Street and Eighth Avenue. Boston Post Road was the name given to the road that ringed North Field. Connected by taxiways to North Field, the 509th compound itself was totally isolated. The gate in the high fence that surrounded the compound was guarded around the clock by armed sentries. Heavily armed MPs patrolled the perimeter of the fence. The living quarters and offices were located inside the secure perimeter. The only air-conditioned buildings in the Pacific were located here. The scientists, technicians and First Ordinance personnel worked here. Crucial parts of the bombs were located here. Anyone trying to gain entrance without authorization could be shot.

The airplanes at North Field were under the same scrutiny. Anyone trying to gain entrance without permission could be shot.

The other B-29 crews on the rest of the island were flying bombing missions every night. They carried maximum bomb loads and enough fuel for the long trip to Japan and back There was one island where they could stop to refuel if necessary on the return flight. Because of the heavy loads. tt was difficult to make a safe takeoff. Sometimes they would lose an engine then crash and explode in the ocean. Struggling to gain altitude on takeoff, the B-29 could be very unforgiving. It was not an uncommon sight to see crashed-out hulks on the island.

Because of the isolation at the north end of the island, there was an undercurrent of ill will toward the 509th. Those brave men still flying nightly missions looked at the 509th as doing nothing for the war effort. Some at the 509th thought that they themselves were destined to finish out the war for an illusionary mission.

*   *   *

TOP SECRET—General Thomas T. Hardy, Acting Chief of Staff, War Department to General Carl Spaatz, Commanding General, United States Army Strategic Air Forces, 25 July 1945.

1. *The 509 Composite 20th Air Force will deliver its first special Bomb as soon as weather will permit visual bombing after 3 August 1945 on one of the targets: Hiroshima, Kokura, Nii-Gata and Nagasaki.*
2. *Additional bombs will be delivered on the above targets as soon as made ready by project staff.*

On July 31 and August 2 1945 thousands of B-29 bombed Japanese cities, Still Japan declared its intention to fight to the death. Japan had been warned of utter devastation of the Japanese homeland unless Japan surrendered unconditionally.(in the Potsdam Proclamation on 26 July 1945).

When the Enola Gay took off from Tinian for Hiroshima, the bomb, "Little Boy" wasn't armed. It was done after a safe takeoff because of the frequency of B=29s crashing on takeoff. However that was not the case with, "Fat Boy ",the bomb that was dropped on Nagasaki. Because of the complex detonation system it was armed when it was loaded into the bomb bay. If it had crashed on takeoff it would have vaporized pilot and crew and all of Tinian.

6 AUGUST 1945

On this date a B-29 named Enola Gay commanded by Colonel Paul Tibbets took off from Tinian Island in the Marianas at 2:10 A.M., flew to Japan and dropped the first atomic bomb on Hiroshima.

TINIAN ISLAND
6 AUGUST 1945

Dearest Mom and Dad:

I just wrote to Cookie and I've reached the conclusion that I should write carbon copies like Dan does. I told Cookie to come over and you will have to exchange letters now and then so I won't have to repeat so many things. I told Cookie about our living quarters, etc.

We aren't on duty yet and it will be quite a few weeks 'cause they have to build a hospital for us first. In the mean time we are enjoying ourselves no end.

No girl is allowed to even walk across the street alone. If some boy wishes to speak with his gal, he calls at headquarters (across the street and around the corner) and headquarters calls our hut on the phone and the girl with the company of another gal goes over to headquarters and the 3 of them chat merrily. If he wishes to take the gal out, he has to get a date for her friend. You always have to go on double dates. When you go out in the eve, you and your escort have to sign out with headquarters together and give your destination. We are allowed to stay out until 10 PM except on party nights when we can stay out until 11. They really protect us here from the men.

Every day we have gone to the beach (properly escorted and signed out). It's marvelous and salty and a beautiful sandy beach. The only trouble is there is lots of coral and you have to wear something on your feet to keep from cutting them. All the guys swim round with a contraption on their faces to look at the coral formations and fish. Can't draw a good picture. So I put the magnifying lenses on and swam around. It's really beautiful and you can hardly believe there are so many little fish swimming around with you in the water. There were some bright blue fish that would look so pretty swimming with your goldfish. I'll send some by the next carrier pigeon.

Met a boy at the beach from Amsterdam, N.Y. and he knows Jean Tiedeman and has been in Delmar several times etc. Small world.

Everyone goes out dating in Jeeps and at 10 PM there are millions of Jeeps lined up outside headquarters, and a line of kids a mile long waiting to sign in.

Last night Ann Romig and an army officer and I with a Marine Corps 1st Lt. went to a buffet supper and dance at one of the air corps officers clubs and had some good food and lots of fun dancing to an orchestra. Hadn't danced in ages, and he was a very good dancer.

You should see the guys stop and stare when we go by in a jeep. Lots of 'em haven't seen a white woman that near in ages. I've seen lots of B-29's and they are really beautiful. We watch large groups of them take off for Tokyo raids. I've seen them at very close range on the ground.

My hair is getting to be a mess. Bathing in the ocean daily and then it never gets dry. Hope the color doesn't change.

The first night after our arrival the 308th men who have been here several weeks, threw a party for all the 308th girls in their club. They had a big cake with "Welcome Home Girls" written on it. I didn't enjoy it very much. I wanted to go to bed but had to wait until the end of the party at 11.

This is such a long letter that I won't be able to use the air mail services.

I've been getting my mail quite promptly. You have been so nice to write so often. I'll try to write as often.

Had a letter from Rev. Brandt which I suppose I should answer so I can mail my request for the County Post.

I suppose I'll have to send you my Christmas list soon. What shall I do about the relatives?

You can put on my list: Sirocco perfume, nail polish, 2 piece short pajamas, and a shower cap. What do you want?

Give my best to anyone you might see that I know. I'll write again later.

Love and besos,

"Pill"

P.S. This island is malaria free for which I am quite relieved.

LETTERS FROM TINIAN 1945

TINIAN ISLAND
8 AUGUST '45

Dearest Mom and Dad:

I'm still alive and kicking and having a wonderful time. As far as dates are concerned, I'm booked up for the rest of the week. What a life! It's a good thing we have to be in early so we always get enough sleep.

What a character I was out with last night!! A major in the air corps. He's been in service quite sometime,—been in England, India, China and now here.

I'll write more often later but I have so many letters to write and there's so much to say.

Don't worry if you don't hear too often. I'm as safe here as anyone could be in the states.

I'm thinking of cutting my hair off one of these days. I'm wearing pigtails at present. The curl just doesn't stay in this heat and it doesn't get dry.

Do you think you would be able to send me some flower seeds to plant when I get in permanent quarter and also some writing paper. Just take it out of my next check.

I have changed my allotment to $100 a month effective September 1. I presume the war bond will still be in effect. I'll let you know later.

Also, Mom, if you are downtown sometime with nothing to do with a few minutes, buy me about 10 birthday cards for future use. I still have a few but not very many. No hurry. Just put it on my bill.

I hope you aren't getting too tired of taking care of my financial affairs. Just let me know if you are. And if you ever need any money for anything whatsoever you know you can have mine. I certainly don't feel that I'm earning it now that I'm not on duty. After all, you always come across when I need money.

Ah well. Guess it's time to write some more letters.

Go to the movies now and then. Maybe I'll be in the newsreel. I'm sure you'll recognize my rain-soaked form under a helmet and behind the dark glasses. Bye for now.

Love,

"Pill"

9 AUGUST 1945

On this date a second atomic bomb is dropped by the United States Army Air Force on Nagasaki, Japan. This B-29 is named "Great Artist", commanded by Major Charles Sweeney, and flown from Tinian Island in the western Pacific.

Also on this date towards midnight, Emperor Hirohito called the Supreme Council together and tried to make the military leaders accept the proposed surrender, but they would not

In his radio address President Truman said the United States had used the atomic bomb "against those who attacked us without warning at Pearl Harbor, against those who have starved and beaten and executed prisoners of war, against those who have abandoned all pretense of obeying international laws of warfare. We have used it to shorten the agony of war, in order to save the lives of thousands and thousands of young Americans. We shall continue to use it until we completely destroy Japan's power to make war. Only a Japanese surrender will stop it."

10 AUGUST 1945

On this date Japan informs the allies that it accepts the surrender terms on the understanding that it does not compromise any demand which prejudices the prerogatives of the Emperor as sovereign ruler.

10 AUGUST '45
TINIAN ISLAND

Dearest Mom and Dad:

Nothing new and different.

Guess the war will soon be over.

Went out with my major again last night. What a character! We are going to a dance Saturday eve and for a tour of the island Sunday P.M. and he wants to book me for the following Tuesday, Thursday, Saturday and Sunday. He's 28, 6 feet tall, reddish blonde hair and homely as—. Can't figure out why he takes me out—don't know if it's the pigtails, my muddy boots or the creaseless slacks. You just can't be neat, clean and feminine on this island.

Went swimming again yesterday PM and it rained most of the afternoon. We had to stay submerged to keep warm. The raindrops were really cold. I didn't get any sunburn. The boys caught a balloon fish and it was really puffed up. Also they caught a sea urchin (porcupine). It was a little larger than a softball. Haven't caught any blue fish for you yet.

In a recent Life magazine there is an article about Guam which shows what our Quonset huts look like. I'm going to take some pictures someday when I find a camera to fit the film I have.

Heard from Floyd today. He is busy instructing WACS. He expects to leave for overseas soon however

Has my mail been coming thru OK? I still don't get a chance to write very often. I wrote to Rev. Brand with my request for the paper.

What do you think of that new bomb?

Is the Empire State Building patched up yet? I'm glad I'm here where it is safe.

What's cooking around Delmar? Hope you all are well and happy and not working too hard. Let me know if I appear in the newsreel.

Nuf said for now.

Gotta wash for chow now. Haven't seen any warm water since I left the states.

They are teaching Spanish here. I've missed 2 classes but I am going to try to attend the rest and see if I can learn anything. It's a 6 week course so I don't know how much use it will be. Something to do anyway.

Love and kisses,

"Pill"

FLOYD

In my 10 August 1945 letter I briefly mentioned Floyd, but he should get more than a brief mention.

Since the bundle of letters my parents saved start in the middle of the Pacific Ocean, a mention should be made that I did write lots of letters prior to going overseas Apparently my parents thought my trip overseas might be a final journey. I never gave it a thought.

While I was stationed at Ft. Monmouth, New Jersey, I did manage to get on the day shift sometimes and was in charge of several wards, and had a Ward Master, Sgt. Floyd Smith of Sherwood, Tenn. He was my right hand man and quite proficient at his job.

We became good friends, but since I was an officer and he was an enlisted man, we weren't allowed to date, "NO FRATERNIZATION".

As a consequence of the rules we had to program times to meet off base to go dancing and eating and enjoy each other. Once I remember taking a bus off the base and meeting to have dinner and dancing the night away. I remember playing the juke box often, especially listening to Frank Sinatra's "Some Other Time"

Floyd even came home to Delmar with me on leave to visit my parents. It was a memorable trip. But all too soon I had signed up for overseas duty and was headed for Europe. We parted as friends and continued to write occasionally.

So a mere mention of Floyd was too little about so good a friend.

LETTERS FROM TINIAN 1945

12 AUGUST '45

Dear Mom and Dad:

S.N.A.F.U.

Here it is Sunday morning with nothing to write. It hasn't rained for over 24 hours. I can't understand it.

It's wonderful to think that Kenny is home safe and sound. He really deserves to be home after all those years over there.

Wish I could have seen the Putnams. They are nice people. Don't you think so? Today is Dave's birthday. I sent him some men's soap when I was at P.O.E.

Last night Ann and I got all sharped up in dresses for the dance last night. We even did our hair up in the morning so we would look nice and surprise the boys. We did too. The club was all decorated special. They had little silver metal cut-outs of B-29s hanging on silver ribbons from the ceiling. Now I have a B-29 hanging over my bed. It is very pretty.

Before the dance we rode over to the field and looked at the B-29s more closely. I'm glad they are on our side.

Today we are going to the tennis matches—Don Budge and some other tennis champs. We're also going to take some pictures—we hope. Some jerk in the signal corps has a big photographers camera and wants me to pose for him—some glamour shots—in pigtails and muddy boots, etc.

Your August 2 airmail arrived yesterday. That's pretty good. Maybe with the new APO they will arrive sooner for all we know. Heard from Elsie, Cookie and Midge in the last couple of days. I wrote to Net and Irving the other day also. I must write to Ithaca one of these days.

If this letter sound jerky, it's the influence of Oscar (Major Roy Oscar—my man this month) and Johnny (Ann's man this month). They are both screwballs and loads of fun. Oscar has a Denman type of humor so we get along. Also at our table was a very handsome yet very young Lt. from Newberg, N.Y. who knows Jane Goewey (remember her?). He sings too—and very, very nicely—better than Sinatra. He is handsome but I'll stick to Oscar, who is homely like Spencer Tracey. If any pictures come out you'll see what I mean.

I'm hoping to get some ironing done this A.M. I am about 10th in line, which is an improvement over yesterday. I was so far down in the line that it never got to me.

You should have read the ships newspaper one Wednesday. It said, "Due to crossing the international date line tomorrow will be Friday". So I am short a Thursday somewhere. Maybe I'll get it back on the return voyage.

Are you going vacationing again soon? I hope so. How about coming here for a weekend? Bring your boots and raincoat.

PAULINE D. WEBB, (LT. PAULINE A. DENMAN, A. N. C. WWII)

Yesterday I saw an automobile. First I've seen in many a day.
That's about all for now.

Love and besos,

"Pill"

ELECTRONIC RASPBERRIES

The allies were able to develop counter radar techniques that had the Germans and Japanese completely confused in the closing months of the war.

Scientists found that the aluminum foil used to wrap gum and cigarettes was a perfect radar fouler-up. The foil technique was developed after ordinary radar wave jamming had lost most of its effectiveness.

The allies used thousands of metallic foil strips, throwing them from high flying planes. They virtually blocked out Nazi attempts to check allied flights. These narrow metallic strips dropped in clusters or in long solid ropes would create a confusing blur on the enemy radar screens. One hundred pounds of shredded foil would give a radar impression of seven hundred bombers.

The military officers said that if Germany had had a similar technique during the Battle of Britian, they might have wiped out the British Isles.

13 AUGUST 1945

On this date the Japanese surrender documents approved by President Truman and sent to General MacAuthur. American aircraft fly over Tokyo and other Japanese cities dropping millions of leaflets explaining the position reached in the surrender negotiations and the true state of affairs in Japan. However, the Japanese "hawks" still refuse to admit defeat.

LETTERS FROM TINIAN 1945

Dearest Mom and Dad:

Here it is washday again and I've done all my washing and my sheets changed. This is just a short letter because I wrote yesterday and not much has passed since then.

Yesterday Oscar (my major again) and I went to the tennis matches and watched four professionals who really know how to push the ball over the net. Maybe you recognize their names. Don Budge, Bob Riggs, Frank Parker and ? Savern or sumpn. We talked with Don Budge and took his picture. We also took pictures elsewhere on the island, B-29s', me Oscar etc. If they come out, you can be expecting them in the mail someday.

Last eve we were going to the Al Pearce Show, but after riding around the island 3 times we couldn't find the right theater so we ended up with the 308th club. This afternoon we are going to the beach if Oscar can get off. He works in the radar business. He used to fly, but "when he found out how dangerous flying was, he took a ground job". He has a sense of humor like Uncle Irving. In fact, you'd like him.

Tonight I am going to my first Spanish class. I'm hoping to make a go of it. Como esta usted? Comprendo?

I still haven't solved the problem of my hair. Jeep riding just doesn't go well 'cause it blows all over the place. And pigtails don't do anything for me. Guess I'll write to Mr. Anthony and have him solve my problem. A lot of the girls have "butch haircuts"—hair 1 ½ inch long all over and usually not curly and looks awful—but it is cool and practical. Yesterday Don Budge almost dropped in his tracks when he saw one of our girls with a haircut like that and a fatigue hat on. His reaction to her caused a delay in the game and a 10 minute roar from the grand stand.

We really have an awful lot of fun. I'll forget how to work when the day arrives. There won't even be time for work.

That's about all for now. How's everything with you?

Love,

"Pill"

PRESENT II

Since the letters make reference to numerous people perhaps it would be more clear or of more interest if I indicated where they came from or where I came from.

This isn't an autobiography, just letters I wrote a long time ago, but some clarification would be helpful. When I pick up a new book to read, the author often introduces so many characters and sometimes refers to them by the first and sometimes the last name thus it does confuse the reader, at least it confuses me, so I write out the names on a slip of paper to keep it clear. A few authors do list the cast of characters at the beginning of the book but it rarely happens.

I was born in Amherst, Massachusettes where my father was teaching at the university, having just earned his Masters in Agricultural Engineering at Cornell. My sister, Marjorie (Midge) was born two years earlier while he was an undergraduate at Cornell in Ithaca, New York.

. He was born in 1885 on a farm outside the city of Ithaca, N. Y. While attending Ithaca High school he drove to school in a horse and buggy, and ate his lunch in the livery stable with his horse. I have a beautiful gold framed picture, about 3 by 4 feet, of him with long blonde curls and a velvet tight fitting suit. He was about twelve and the photo was to mark the occasion of the cutting off of the curls that I now have in among my special things.

My mom was born in Vermont in 1893 and was also a teacher. They met at a dance in rural Vermont where he was teaching summer school. During the time I knew them, my parents never went dancing, nor did they ever go out. I don't ever remember my parents having a baby sitter for me,

Dad's brother Irving, (O'Bean) went to veterinary college at Cornell. Dad said he went to Ag School instead of veterinary because he liked the lab facilities better! How different our lives might have been if he had done as his brother had and studied veterinary medicine.

As a child, I never wanted to start going to school and used to scribble on books and say if I had to go to school, that is what I would do. Of course I went to school, starting in a one room school house in Hathorne, Mass, where my dad was teaching at Essex Aggie School.

In my letters from Tinian I mention, Midge and Dave. Midge went to school in Delmar, New York, and Dave in Elsmere, New York two villages outside Albany , N.Y., the capitol. While in elementary school The American Legion awarded a medal to the outstanding student in each school. Midge won the medal in Delmar, and Dave in Elsmere. However they never met until the schools were consolidated as Bethlehem Central High School in Delmar.

I was in seventh grade when I first saw Dave and ultimately had a huge crush on him, so when he suddenly appeared on our front porch one day, I was so surprised that I went and hid upstairs. He was calling on Midge, (unexpedly) and she had just washed her hair and didn't look too great at least not for receiving a gentleman caller. Prior to that visit I had sent him a Valentine, signed, "P. Denman".

>What every young boy should know
>How to make the dough
>If you liked me enough to learn
>I'm sure my true love
>You could earn

Was he calling on the wrong girl? Well about eight years later he married her.

In my letters I mention "Cookie", who was Jane Thomson. She was and is a very important person in my life. We were friends in high school and when as a senior I had no idea what to do with my life after graduation, Jane said she was going in nurses training, so I decided to do the same and we went in together at the same school.

I am so very thankful that I studied nursing because of the various turns of events in my life. I had a career to which I could turn, that would allow me to find work in my field wherever I went. First in the Army Nurse Corps during the war. Then later with my R. N. in New York state I had reciprocity with Rhode Island and Florida where I later found work. I owe it all to "Cookie"

14 AUGUST 1945

On this date Emperor Hirohito assembled the Imperial Council and decided that his rescript shall be transmitted by radio announcing the acceptance of unconditional surrender.

On receipt of the news of the surrender, the Americans got ready to occupy Japan. At 7 PM President Truman announced "it" was over. Peace at last.

Dearest Mom and Dad:

It is 9 A.M. (15th Aug.) here and we have just heard the wonderful news. It's impossible to believe it is an actuality.

Last night we watched hundreds of Superforts return from what must be the last raid, thank goodness. We were sitting on the terrace of the Coral Club, under the stars last night watching their return.

We haven't been swimming for 5 days because they are dredging the coral etc. out of the beach to make it better for swimming. But Oscar came over anyway and we took tours of the island, played Ping-pong at the club, etc.

Our greatest discomfort here is being thirsty and being unable to quench it. The water is lukewarm and not too tasty. The best thing is the iced lemonade at the club. At meals we usually have pink lemonade, coffee or something to kill the taste of the water. Haven't had any milk since the middle of last month. My teeth will be falling out.

Heard from Ginnie Beinkafner the other day. She and Bookie are vacationing now. You are too aren't you?

There is so much noise and celebration on the part of some of the girls that it is difficult to concentrate. Maybe I should join them but I'm getting old.

Are you getting tired of hearing about Oscar? I see him 3 times a day. He comes over at 11:30 AM during his lunch hour, then he comes over for the afternoon, then he comes over and we go out every evening. He's an awfully nice guy. He takes pictures of me all over the place, but they won't be good 'cause I'm always in slacks, dark glasses and bandana. The slacks look terrible because of no cleaners and unavailability of irons.

Someday I am going to take some pictures out by the washroom, etc. showing how we wash out of our helmets, etc.

That's enough. Incidentally the Flier from Newberg is on his way home and he says he is going to call you up. His name is Tom Williams and is a roommate of Oscar's, who kept wanting Oscar to let me go out with him, which I didn't 'cause I like Oscar. Whether he'll call or not I don't know, but I thought I'd warn you.

Love and kisses,

Pill

17 AUGUST 1945

On this date General Prince Higashikumi becomes the Prime Minister of Japan and forms a new government.

17 AUGUST 1945
TINIAN ISLAND

Dearest Mom and Dad:

Well, the war has been officially over for several days now, but what is in store for us we don't know, except that we may get new orders with in the next two weeks. It is difficult to even guess what our next move will be.

I went to Spanish class again last night and I enjoy it very much. Hope I can learn something.

Today I was ironing around 11:00 AM and I heard the Contented Hour on the radio. Seems funny to hear eve programs in the AM. I haven't used my radio at all because I can't plug it in anywhere except the ironing room when no one is ironing, and there almost always is someone ironing. From outward appearances there is nothing broken.

This later is a mess 'cause I'm lying in bed. I have a date with Roy (Oscar) in 10 minutes so I better get dressed. I can't keep a major waiting. Yesterday he brought me some ice cream. The first I've had since I was on the ship. Roy keeps me so busy that I just can't get any letters written. Received your August 5th letter, Dad, today.

Hope you enjoyed your second week of vacation. Don't worry about me. I don't have time to be lonesome or unhappy. Please have fun and don't work too hard.

Love and kisses,

"Pill"

20 AUGUST 1945

On this date the Japanese delegation returned to Tokyo with the Allied dispositions for the occupation and for the signature of the surrender

The nurse and the major

21 AUGUST 1945
HAPPY BIRTHDAY MOM

Dearest Mom and Dad:

While I am awaiting the arrive of ever faithful Roy Oscar, I shall drop you a hurried note. The above drawing is not original. I copied it from some the chaplain had. It is quite typical except for the palm tree. I've seen none at all on this island. I've seen banana trees but no bananas. Tough?! The island is Saipan as we see it from here. From some places on this island you can't see the ocean separating the two and it appears like all one island.

Today the Seabees are busy paving the road in front of our "house". The base is about a foot depth of coral and it is so white that it appears like snow and almost blinds you as snow does on a bright day. The Seabees are all that they say. They really construct things but fast. One day there is a piece of land and no building—next day there is a quonset.

This morning at 3 AM there was quite a lot of excitement. The enlisted men's mess hall, bakery and storeroom went up in flames. Such a fire I never did see. It was as near to us as Mansfields' house to ours. The sparks were flying in our direction and we all were outside with pajamas and flashlights watching the fire spread and rise to the sky. Two wooden water towers—our supply—were within two feet of the burning building and I can't understand what saved it. Everyone went and filled their canteens just in case. Water to us is vital.

We won't be able to go to the beach for about another 5 days. Can't wait until they get it fixed. Imagine with all this ocean—and we can't go in. There are other beaches but "off limits" to women bathers.

We went to the movies the other night, and amazing as it may seem, it didn't rain once during the entire showing. If the picture became boring we would watch the stars or the B-29s' or the lights on Saipan, or the frogs jumping on someone, producing screams from the gals. Lizards, a couple of inches long, crawl along now and then. Today in the barracks there were several large spiders (bodies about 1—1 ½ inches in diameter) annoying all those present.

Life on this little island continues to prove interesting. One night a sergeant under the influence of alcohol crawled under our fence and was immediately apprehended by our efficient M.P.'s. What chance does one Sgt. have while 50 women scream and turn on their flashlights? Never a dull moment in our barracks. We are well guarded and protected from anything.

Guess this is enough ambling. Cookie wrote that Bob is on his way home. I certainly hope everything goes well for them. She has been so lonely for so long. She is getting everything ready for her wedding now. Wish I could be there.

Be good, keep happy

Love, Pauline.

24 AUGUST

TINIAN

Dearest Mom and Dad:

According to my records I haven't written to you in three days. That is pretty bad.

Roy and I managed to get a couple of rolls of film developed but not printed. In the event that we do get them printed I will send some to you immediately. Am going to take some more pictures around here in a few days.

Heard from Mrs. Ferguson. Doug's ship was badly damaged near Okinawa, but he is safe. Don't know if he was injured or not.

Elsie is vacationing now and Cookie is rushing like mad getting ready for a wedding. I am doing the usual things. The beach is still closed. I certainly will be glad when it opens again. Haven't been in for two weeks.

I'm still taking Spanish and if I study a little now and then I may make out all right.

Still haven't heard any word of orders concerning our unit yet.

I have to go and take a shower now and get sharped up for Roy He'll be here in another hour.

Thanks for writing so often. Thank you dad for the crossword puzzles. Roy and I do them together. We also play gin rummy, Cribbage and "Sink It". We have lots of fun. He is such a nice fellow. I'm sure you'd like him.

Love,

Pill

DOUG

Since I have mentioned Doug and his mom, Mrs Ferguson in these letters, I should elucidate about him. While he was a student at Rensselaer Polytechnic Institute in Troy, N.Y., he came down with pneumonia and was quite critical in our hospital where I was a student nurse. I became well acquainted with him and his family.

After his recovery we started dating and in due time he gave me his fraternity pin. I went home with him to Cleveland, Ohio at Christmas. The trip was quite memorable as it was wartime and the trains were crowded with standing room only as the rule , the isles were packed with soldiers. We were lucky to have a seat at all and together.

His parents became very fond of me and I them. I am sure they were disappointed when I chose not to marry, but to join the Army Nurse Corps. He was a Naval Ensign and soon would be assigned to duty.

Shortly after my return to civilian life in Delmar, I had a call from Douglas. He and his father were in Albany and wanted me to join them for dinner and dancing afterward at their hotel. It was a pleasant evening, and that was our last encounter. I remember very little about that visit and what I gleaned about his life. I wish I could remember.

OPENING
HELLBIRD

OFFICERS CLUB

TINIAN *27 AUGUST 1945*

28 AUGUST

Dearest Mom and Dad:

I better get on the ball and write some letters. You have been so wonderful in writing so often. Heard from Kenny Van Alstyne today. He's very happy to be at home and well he might be. He doesn't like the idea of going back to work.

I'm O.D. this evening so Roy is back in his area at the movies. It's the first eve I've been in since landing on Tinian. And it surely seems strange. And tonight is our 3rd anniversary. We have been going together 3 weeks. He's an awfully nice fellow, but of course I'm, no more serious than I've ever been with anyone. Guess it just isn't for me. He may be going home in a couple of weeks. Woe is me.

Last night I skipped Spanish class to go to a big party—the opening of "The Hell birds Officers Club". It was so crowded and so many stags that Roy and I didn't enjoy it at all. It's a very nice club, most of it including the dance floor is outside. Fortunately it didn't rain until after we got home. It had rained all day up to the time of the party, amazing as it may seem.

It has been raining constantly night and day since Sunday. Can't seem to get anything dry. Hope it lets up soon, but they say September is the rainiest month so maybe we are in for it.

So you finally located this little island on a map. Not very impressive huh! I like it here however. Maybe I won't like it so well after Roy leaves. Of course there are thousands of other men here . . . But Roy is quite honest and faithful and has a lot of gray matter under his thinning red hair. We write letters to each other every day—even though we see each other 3 times a day. Crazy aren't we?

Last night I was awakened around 3:30 A.M. and had to go to the latrine. I walked the length of the quonset to the door and was too scared to venture outside so I returned to bed to wait for daylight. What a life—I'm too used to modern conveniences. Imagine wearing a raincoat and rubbers to go to the bathroom. I guess you can imagine.

Dad, do you still drive all those young gals to work yet? You'd really miss 'em I bet. I enjoy all the little clipping you send. Roy and I always do the crossword puzzles together. He's a cross between you, Dad, and Uncle Irving. Maybe that's why I like him. He's awfully nice to me. He has a sense of humor like ours.

That's about all for now. Have so many other letters to answer that I don't know where to begin.

I'll be good and write more often. I'll let you know as soon as I hear anything concerning our future activities or moves.

Love and kisses,

Pill

ASSIGNMENT
OR CHORES

There we were on Tinian, a large group of well educated Registered Nurses eager to help out in the war but with no assignments to duty. The Army got us there but were hard put to know what to do with us I am sure. They at least housed us and fed us and protected us. Of course they couldn't prevent the pilots from flying low over our shower room, a tent—like enclosure with no roof. I saw plenty of B-29s with PW in big letters painted on their undersides for (" Prisoners of War") flying very low

For chores we were required to look after our own space, cot and bedside table (orange crate), our personal laundry and our bodies. We had occasional assignments, i. e. latrine duty (clean it), sweep the front office, sweep the Quonset, O. D. (officer of the day), etc Otherwise we were on our own to entertain ourselves within our compound leaving only when properly escorted and signed out.

We had our own dining hall/recreation room and could invite friends in when properly signed in and invited

*   *   *

I assume there must have been an area for the prisoners of war but we knew nothing of it. There was a compound on the island for the ":gooks." , as they were called, the Japanese Tinian natives who had worked in the sugar cane fields so maybe that is where all the PWs were kept. We were not briefed on many things , things that we didn't need to know

So there we were with no radio, TV, computers, newspapers or any of the sources we have today. We had no good source of the world at large or of our little world, just "latrine rumors"

We were on vacation on a Pacific Isle, so enjoy! However we knew there was a war going on. We heard the planes overhead constantly, going on missions.or returning to base. We often saw large columns of black smoke on the horizon and knew another plane had crashed on take off or when trying to land. We knew there were still Japanese in caves on the island who hadn't yet surrendered and sometimes you heard of one coming out of a cave with arms raised in surrender

LETTERS FROM TINIAN 1945

30 AUGUST

Dearest Mom and Dad:

Someday soon I may be able to mail some pictures to you. Maybe in another week they will be ready. Won't guarantee any masterpieces. The uniform of this island is "sloppy". With the available washing facilities, heat and rain, there is no alternative.

Yesterday it was sunny almost all day so we went to the beach again. Today the rain is pouring down in buckets. I just don't do my hair up any more. I rinse it under the shower every morning when I wash and does it ever feel wonderful. It usually dries in 1—2 hours and has enough natural page boy to look pretty good—for Tinian.

Have Spanish class again tonight. Hope I didn't miss too much by skipping class Monday. By hook or by crook I'll learn the language.

Yesterday we had to fill out a questionnaire, asking for 5 choices of subjects to study. They are starting, sometime, an educational program to occupy the soldier's spare duty time. After the last war the soldier had a lot of spare duty hour with nothing to do—so they told us—and they are trying to eliminate that problem by giving classes. Seems like an excellent idea. Of course I've forgotten how to study.

Roy is due to arrive in 12 minutes unless it is still raining on his side of the island. It's such a small island you'd think it would rain all over instead of one area. This morning I looked over at Saipan and the central part was completely obliterated by the rain. Only the extreme right and left tip of the island was visible.

Yesterday at the beach with the help of some binoculars I looked over on Saipan and I could distinguish building, planes, jeeps, etc. But I didn't see Tyrone Power.

You asked if I wanted you to send any clippings from my papers. You don't need to bother. I should be getting it soon out here I hope. I wrote to the minister right after arriving here.

Must be a native of New York City named the streets here. The main highway is Broadway and the streets that cross it are named numerically.

Love and kisses,

Pill

31 AUGUST '45

Dearest Mom and Dad:

Just a hurried note before "lights out". Got the enclosed pictures tonight and want to send them right off to you. I'll have some more in a few days.

Today I had the detail of cleaning the shower room. It took an hour and I got my back sunburned. By hook or by crook I shall get tan.

Nothing new here. Roy and I are going to try and get a tennis court reserved and play a few sets.

Nite now.

Love, Pill

2 SEPTEMBER 1945
THE SURRENDER OF JAPAN

The ceremonies took less than a half hour to complete. It was the formal signing of the surrender of Japan more than two weeks after accepting the Allies terms. The signing took place on the battleship USS Missouri, anchored in Tokyo Bay with other United States' and British ships.

3 September 1945
Labor Day Anniversary—
10 months in the army.

Dearest Mom and Dad:

Still no news, but now that V-J day is officially proclaimed things may begin popping. Last night the 10 P.M. curfew was raised 'till 11 P.M. If any of us are late, our escort's name is taken and turned into the General. I bet no one will be late around here now.

I'm still taking Spanish. The class that I skipped last Monday was postponed because of no electricity in the classroom. Lucky me.

Went to the beach yesterday and got a nice pink tinge to my entire (almost—bathing suits being what they are) body. Roy fell asleep on the beach and when he woke up he didn't know where he was—then he saw me and called "Pill", grabbed me and kissed me, knocking my bandana and sunglasses off. What a character. He was due to go stateside this week but he got a 30 day extension, and is going to try for another if I'm still here. He's crazy.

This surely is a funny world. When I was a civilian at home, I was saying good-bye to the boys who were going overseas. Now I am overseas and I'm saying good-bye to the boys who are going home and get discharged. What a life!

The other day a fellow was picking bananas and 4 Japs came out of the bushes with their hands over their heads, surrendering. Now the boy gets an award for capturing 4 Japs. Probably a story. Anything for interest here on the island. Last night I dreamed I was in Seattle, and I was looking for Lyn's family but just couldn't find them.

Roy is really like a father to me. Would he ever be mad if I told him that! The other night I had to go to the latrine and didn't know where it was, so Roy borrowed a flashlight and went outside to hunt for it; then he came back and got me and led me almost to the door. Then he waited for me up by the club. I'm sure the censor enjoys these revelations of mine.

Am enclosing a couple more snaps which aren't very clear. Don't know whether it was the fault of the film or the printer. Film doesn't keep too well in this warm damp climate.

There doesn't seem to be much else of interest to write about.

Love,

Pauline

5 Sept.

Dearest Mom and Dad:

Just a very short hurried letter to let you hear from me.

Got 4 letters today. One from Dad, Midge and Dave, Alyce and Mac and Floyd (who is now a **Sgt.**) He's still in the states but expects to ship out soon anyway.

No news here of any kind. Played tennis for a little while yesterday—too hot to finish the set. Then we went swimming—the beach is nice—you can swim and dive with no danger.

Got an orange crate yesterday to use as a bedside table. Decorated it with 2 white hand (not Turkish) towels and the scraps I have with me from my evening gown. Looks rather cute. Ann Romig gave me some yard goods to use as a bedspread so my little area is a little bit homey.

Please forgive the shortness of this letter. I have so many to write and so little time. Am still having lots of fun. Hope you are doing the same. Heard from Alta, too.

Love,

Pill

P. S Enclosed item you may find interesting.

COMPLAINT LETTER FROM STATESIDE NEWSPAPER

While on Tinian during the war, we were idle as the hospital had not yet been built. We were there at that time because we were shipped there. We were idle not by choice. Word got back stateside of our situation. The following letters from a newspaper in Maryland came into my possession:

Tinian Nurses

To the 29 Tinian GI's—in defense of the A. N. C.

So we're not needed or wanted? Sorry, Bud, but we nurses are on these Pacific "Rocks" for the same reason you are—we were ordered to report at these places for duty.

Certainly, we admit that anyone can take a temperature, see that the ward is clean, etc. But look Bud, you garrison troops can thank God you've never needed much more than that. Perhaps you've never been in a position to need a skilled, trained, woman's care. Ask the boys who know—ask them what they thought of the care they got from the Army nurses. By the boys who know, I mean the casualties from the various Pacific campaigns.

I have been in a position to give care to a fairly large number of these boys and I have had the satisfaction of knowing that they appreciate our work.

As for the clubs—we didn't ask for them. And as for being waited on at table—its an old privilege given officers. We'd gladly eat cafeteria style. We didn't ask to be waited upon.

You can be thankful, boys, we don't seem to have much more to do than take temperatures and see that hospital standards are maintained. When the medical department and we nurses included, doesn't seem to be doing such a spectacular job its good news. It means there are fewer GIs wounded or sick.

And now may I ask, what great and glorious good are you 29 GIs doing on Tinian?

ARMY NURSE

*   *   *

It seems there are a few EM who are bitter at the entire Nurse Corps because they haven't been dated by them or had a chance to flirt with them. Well I am just another GI who has never dated a nurse. Yet my opinion of them is quite different from that of the 29 Tinian GIs.

I have spent quite a bit of time in hospitals, both at home and overseas, and brother, when you are in the depths of despair it really means something to have a nurse around to watch over you and give you a smile. My hat is off to the Army Nurse Corps. We couldn't have done without them at any time during this bloody war that recently has ended.

PVT. LEO KAHN (and one other)

Tinian Nurses

PICTURE POSTCARD OF A BEACH
SEPT. '45

Dearest Mom and Dad,

This looks like our beach. The water's fine. Want to come along?

Nothing new to tell, as always. Guess we are awaiting orders again.

That's all I've ever done in the army.

Love,

Pill

HEADQUARTERS
821ˢᵗ HOSPITAL CENTER
APO #247 —POSTMASTER
San Francisco, California

MEMORANDUM: 6 SEPTEMBER 1945

NUMBER 9:

SECURITY REGULATIONS FOR SERVICE CONNECTED WOMEN

Reference: (a) Cir 19, Hq Iscom, 3 Sep 45

1. The following definitions and instructions supplement Reference a, the provisions of which remain in effect except as modified herein:

    a. Visiting hours at the main Officers' Club, 303d General Hospital, for guests of service women shall begin at 0900 and shall terminate at 2245.

    b. Women are permitted to leave their quarters area on "dates" only after 1200. They may visit their unit area or proceed on official business after 0800.

    c. For daylight hours (0800-1700) the term "Proper Escort" is defined as two women accompanied by an authorized general hospital driver or a male officer. For night hours (1800-2300) the term "Proper Escort" is defined in paragraph 1d (2), Reference a.

    d. Women will be properly escorted at all times and will be in the constant presence of one or more women except during daylight hours when in their unit area and the 303d General Hospital Area and except as provided in paragraph 1d (1), Reference a.

    e. Slacks or skirts will be worn at all times except that women having engagements and leaving the 303dGeneral Hospital Area after 1700 will wear skirts. Shorts are permitted to be worn in quarters or on tennis courts, providing that slacks are worn while being transported to and from the tennis courts. Rolling up of trouser legs higher than six inches is prohibited except during athletic contests held in unit areas.

    f. Women on detached service and temporary duty are subject to the rules and regulations of the unit to which attached for such duty.

    g. Visits to ships in Tinian Harbor and fishing trips are authorized when women are properly escorted.

    h. Hospital Commanders are not authorized to grant permission to any personnel for air travel.

Memo. 9, Hq 821st Hosp Center, 6 Sep 45, cont'd

    i. Restricted areas (see Incl, Cir 19, Hq Isccm, 3 Sep 45): Women will not visit restricted areas under any circumstances.

2. The above instructions and rules will be observed by all nurses, female dieticians, physiotherapy aides, and female Red Cross workers assigned to or quartered by units of this command.

BY ORDER OF COLONEL HOLCOMBE
W. M. Johnson, Capt.MAC

How strange that we get these orders for proper conduct after we have been here a month and the war is over, etc.,. " Situation normal, all fouled up"!! SNAFU

LETTERS FROM TINIAN 1945

Dear Mom and Dad

Will try to make this letter a little longer than the last. Just got in from the beach. They now have a public address system at the beach and we have music while we swim. More fun. Tonight maybe we will go to a movie. Haven't been in a long time. There haven't been any good pictures lately.

Roy is helping me with my Spanish. He got a book from the library and we study an hour each day together. I have learned to count to 100 now and hope to learn lots more now that he is helping me.

Now that we have been here so long, I can tell a little about our trip that I wasn't able to mention before. We stopped in Honolulu. We sighted land just at sunup so we saw the sun rise over the island. It was very beautiful. It was really nice to see land again after being away for several days at sea. It was a beautiful sight. We stayed at the dock and could see the city and the houses in the hills and the Aloha tower. We stayed until 6 P.M.(we weren't allowed off the boat), and as we pulled out of the harbor orchestra music drifted up to us—it was "Aloha—O" (excuse spelling) and it made it seem very sad, especially when it also meant we were heading away from our country. (If I told you this stuff in one of the last few letters—skip it). The clock in the Aloha tower was not going—it stopped during the attack on Pearl Harbor in '41. Now that the war is over (what a wonderful phrase) it probably has been started up again.

Our next stop was at Eniweton in the Marshalls—we anchored so far away that we didn't see the island. We picked up our orders there. (We stayed a few hours).

Our next stop was Guam. We went right into the harbor and stayed 1 1/2 days.

We didn't get off there, although some landed there from our ship. The harbor is beautiful and very active. Our next and last stop was here. When we first stopped here it looked very bleak and uninhabited (although we had heard it was a big air corps base.)

When we left the good ole' USA the Red Cross was there with coffee and donuts and a band played for us. What an exciting experience—actually going up the gangplank all loaded down with everything. Ours backs were killing us 'cause our musette bags were loaded with everything that did't fit in our hand luggage

Just got in from supper. We had ice cream!!! First time in many long weeks. We ate it first before it melted.

Life is going on around here about as usual. I'm awaiting word from Cookie concerning Bob's arrival, a wedding or whatever else the story is.

Ann (my friend) just joined a camera club so we are taking pictures of everything and everybody. She will also be doing her own printing and developing. The man who prints pictures in our area here charges 10¢ per print and does very poor work, so Ann can print pictures for us.

PAULINE D. WEBB, (LT. PAULINE A. DENMAN, A. N. C. WWII)

My county post hasn't started to come yet but am keeping my eye open for it. I always enjoy reading about what's going on at home

We haven't had mail in several days so am expecting some today. Haven't heard from Hazel since I was first in Bragg. Wonder where she is and what she is doing.

Heard from Mrs. Fergusen again the other day. She enclosed a newspaper article written about Doug's ship. The ship was very badly damaged off Okinawa and just managed to limp back stateside for repairs. About 100 of the crew were killed, wounded or blown overboard. Doug didn't get a scratch

He. was home for a few weeks—he had a mustache.

I'd just as soon dispense with exchanging Christmas with the relatives. It will be hard to know what to send me. I'll leave it up to you to make the decision and proceed accordingly. If we do exchange you will have to do my shopping for me since you can't get anything over here. It really doesn't make a bit of difference to me either way. I think I can take care of Midge and Dave, you and Dad, Cookie and Elsie, unless I specify otherwise later.

Some more things I could use for gifts ,: Cologne—"Tweed", "A' bientot", and stockings (tan) 9½ and mascara—did I tell you that before—I need that now.

Your air mail arrives much faster than the other way. I think my mail reaches you faster than yours reaches me. Air mail seems the only sensible thing.

You sound as if you had such a nice time in Rochester. Isn't Alyce's brother good looking? Dad, did you enjoy the monkeys in the zoo?

I'll write you as soon as the package arrives.

Oscar is from Detroit. He expects to be going home soon. Guess he plans to go to University of Michigan on his return and get his Master's degree. He's very intelligent and very nice, and wonderful to me. He's an only child and his dad died in the last war. He has a stepfather. I don't think he had a very happy childhood

I doubt very much if we will be heading for home soon. I think our next move will be west or northwest. Time will tell. We haven't done what we came overseas to do, and I'd like to do something before I return.

You certainly have lots of peaches. So do we. Almost every day for dessert, alternating with canned fruit salad, sliced pears and sliced pineapples.

That's about enough gab for now.

Love, Pill

12 SEPTEMBER

Dear Mom and Dad:

This is purely a business letter. I'm enclosing a money order for sixty ($60.00) dollars. Last night Roy and I celebrated our 5th anniversary (5 week). It rained cats and dogs all evening. We played cribbage, black jack and chatted. We usually go to our own club, the 308th, because we have unrationed cokes there and free lemonade. Living expenses here on Tinian are very low. All I buy is candy bars and cigarettes now and then, and stamped envelopes.

Tonight they tell me that Alan Ladd is appearing in person at our theater here. Maybe we'll go, if we can get near the place.

Heard from Hazel yesterday, also a nice letter from Aunt Margaret. Hazel wrote the letter July 15 and was still at Fort Dix. Maybe she won't get out of there at all.

That's all for now. Be good, have fun, and keep happy.

Love,

Pill

16 SEPTEMBER
TINIAN ISLAND
SUNDAY EVE

Dear Mom and Dad:

'Bout time I wrote!

There are several things to report. Gerald Grimm came over here to see me the other day. Was I ever surprised! He said he thought he saw me at the beach a few weeks ago, but it seemed quite remote so he didn't approach me. Then his wife or someone wrote that I was in the 308th and since he is with the 304th which is also here he immediately took steps to look me up. Small world. He came over for a little while this afternoon. He brought over some pictures of Sandy and the baby.

Last night we went to a club opening and it was quite a gala affair. A seventeen piece orchestra and a magnificent club. The clubs over here are more beautiful than some of the best clubs in N.Y.C.—BUT the most wonderful thing about the club — A ladies powder room right in the building with a ***flush toilet***, wash bowl and two mirrors. All the girls spent the majority of the evening flushing the darn thing. What an experience—and privacy too. First time since leaving the ship.

The other night we went to an opening of a smaller club—but the latrine situation was nil. Six of us girls had to be convoyed in jeeps by 2 male officers to a men's latrine about 3/4 of a mile away. The boys had to stand guard outside to avoid any mishaps—and to top it off we got caught in a very heavy shower on the return trip. Very embarrassing. Ah, life on Tinian.

We went to a tea dance this afternoon and had a nice time—orchestra and all. We are going to a movie tonite I guess. We've been dancing so much that we are all tired out.

Heard today that we can mention that our destination is a place in Japan south of Tokyo. Don't know how many weeks it will be before we leave. You know how slow we've been about moving before.

It's toss up who will leave first—Roy or I. I'll miss him a lot. We've had so much fun together.

Just got in. We went to see "Bring on the Girls". Didn't we see that together, Mom? I knew I'd seen it before, but it was enjoyable to see a good colored musical comedy again. We had 2 showers during the picture but we had our raincoats so it wasn't bad. Just got my glasses a little wet.

That's about all for now.

MONDAY A.M.

My County Post hasn't started to arrive yet.

PAULINE D. WEBB, (LT. PAULINE A. DENMAN, A. N. C. WWII)

Roy is from Detroit. He expects to leave for the states soon. Has put in an application to go to M.I.T. for a year under Army sponsorship and study radar and radio. He is an electrical engineering grad. The course at M.I.T. starts in November so he doesn't know if he will make it or not. If he does it means he will be in the army 3 more years.

When we joined the army, we signed up for the duration of the emergency plus 6 months. The emergency can last for 10 years. One never knows. But the other day they had a paper for those interested to sign. Those who signed would be the ones who would stay in for the duration plus 6 months—by signing it they cancelled all their points and any eligibility for discharge. About 7 girls out of 80 signed. I didn't, but I don't know how long I will be in. I have 12 points, and a job in Japan soon. I'm quite excited about going there. They say the damage in Tokyo and other cities is unbelievable. Those B-29's are wonderful planes, and my radar man helped win the war.

The enclosed picture is of the club we went to Saturday. The picture doesn't do the place justice at all. You should see the entrance on the other side. Looks like a colonial mansion with a big lobby like a theater with murals, statues, etc. Even the general was there at the dance.

Bye for now.

Love,

Pill

P.S. You can keep sending the crossword puzzles. So glad Cookie's Bob is home. Am anxious to hear more about it.

The 10 P.M. curfew is still in effect. It's about time they lifted it to 11 P.M. No other news now. I'll be writing again soon

102

FORMAL OPENING
58th BOMB WING OFFICERS CLUB
Tinian   15 September 1945

PAULINE D. WEBB, (LT. PAULINE A. DENMAN, A. N. C. WWII)

In my letters to my parents I mention the opening of new clubs on the island but make no mention of what was served for pleasant libation. My dad would write and inquire if they were opening any churches. He was a rather strict person and did not drink or smoke. So I never mentioned the system the army had for providing alcoholic beverages.

Each week (or less often?) we would sign up for what we wanted to order and we would then take our own bottles with us to the clubs. A BYOB system.

On one occasion I received a phone call at our Quonset hut from a gentleman telling me that *they didn't have the item I ordered and that all they had was Del Prado Rum. I was a bit befuddled because I knew very little about bottled alcoholic beverages. So the man admitted that he was Roy just teasing me. So Del Prado Rum was always a joke we shared. I do not know if there is such a product.*

So that is one of the things I remember after all these years, and I have no idea about that rum, is it or was it a real brand?..

A PICTURE POST CARD
19 SEPT

Dear Folks,

Just a note to say , "Hello". Everything is fine and dandy. Roy is still here with me and will be for a while yet. Is Cookie married yet? Hope she is as happy as she expected.

Love, Pill

PICTURE POSTCARD
22 SEPT

Dear Mom and Dad,

Am getting ready for another big party tonight. Presume Cookie is very busy, haven't heard from her, Elsie has written however. Jack Cassell is in Hawaii and is expecting to come to Tinian. Roy and I are still having wonderful times together. Had a V-mail from Net and O'bean. They are quite busy. No more room.

Love, Pill

V-MAIL

"Victory Mail" or "V-Mail" was created by the government to speed up the delivery time and allow more room in overseas shipping. Letters were written on pre-printed envelope sheets that could be photographed and transferred to microfilm for mailing.

On the next page is a sample of V-Mail compared to a regular envelope

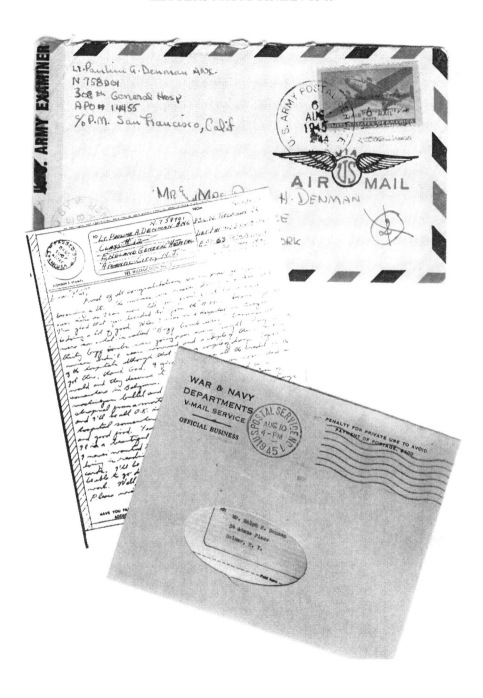

LETTERS FROM TINIAN 1945

MONDAY ON TINIAN
24 SEPT.

Dear Mom and Dad:

I certainly have neglected my letter writing these days. Am anxiously awaiting word from Cookie re Bob and the wedding. Elsie has written but I don't know when the wedding is to be. From what Elsie says, they are both very happy. They have every right to be after waiting so long.

The flower seeds arrived 2 days after the letter. I'll try to get a letter off to Mrs. Washburn some time. I still haven't been getting my Albany County Post.

Today we had a first in a series of lectures concerning Japan. It is required for all who are going to Japan—and we might as they say now.

Did I tell you Jack Cassell is in Hawaii and comes to Tinian next? Roy says for me to let him know when Jack arrives so he can stay home. He thinks I'd go out with Jack. He's crazy. Incidently Roy told me that he is engaged to a girl in the states. So Roy is in a mess because he doesn't want to marry the girl and she is getting her clothes all ready for a wedding. That's not my problem—he can figure it out himself.

Saturday night was the opening of the club of Roy's Bomb Wing and it was a gala affair except for the fact that there were 2,000 people present and only 50 women. Trying to dance was a problem. When they had a tag dance, I'd never dance more than two steps at a time. Was I ever worn out. I felt like a USO girl. All of us girls went limping to the ladies room—which is by far the nicest ladies room on the island. Flush toilet—a mirror about 6 feet by 6 feet, dressing table with 2 benches, linoleum floor, quilted walls—what a beautiful room.

We have been to the opening of seven officers' clubs and are going to another opening tonight. Don't know why they keep opening new clubs. Every one is different and the architectural design of some are really out of this world. I think there is going to be a great change in clubs in the states when these boys get back stateside. I have some candid shots taken with one of the club openings which I'll be showing you when I get home.

Last night we went to the movies and saw "Brewsters Millions" in the rain. One afternoon we took a tour of the island and took pictures all over everywhere again. We went to the site of our hospital. Of course all work is stopped now since the hospital won't be needed here. It almost broke my heart to think that the hospital will never be finished. It was to be located on the best site on the island. The nurses quarters were finished and were very nice. If only it could have come into existence I would have loved working there and I could have planted my flowers under my window. It would have been the most ideal set up in the army.

Had another letter from Mrs. Ferguson and enclosed 2 pictures of Doug with his mustache and he looks terrible. He looks very hard and bitter and unhappy. He was home again early this month. He and his dad went up into Michigan to go fishing, while poor Mrs. Ferguson stayed home and did her canning. You women always get stuck with the canning. Don't think I'll ever be a wife and mother. There is too much to do. Life on Tinian is certainly making me lazy.

Remember my ANC dress that I wore at home quite frequently? It is washable, in fact it launders beautifully, even in cold water, and irons with sprinkling. I dreaded washing it for fear it would shrink or lose its shape. Since we can't wear slacks in the eve, all I have to wear is that dress, and my shirts and one skirt. The tropical skirt is washable too. I certainly wish I'd purchased a beige suit when I was in the states. Everyone said it was foolish to get them, so very few of us bought them, but the few that did are the lucky ones. The beige skirt and crispy starched white shirt really look sharp and it is a welcome change no doubt.

Can't think of anything else to include on my Christmas list and birthday list. Do you think you could possible pick out a pair of brown pumps for me and send them? If you think it difficult don't bother. In case you should—you could use my spectator pumps for a guide. Not the new ones I had last summer but the old brown and white ones—the size is the same and the heel is right. For Army wear they will have to have the toes and heels present, no bows. Understand? If you think it will be too difficult, don't try. Only a suggestion—but send them not for Christmas—take it out of a check.

How are you both feeling these days? In the pink I hope. Eva, one of the girls here that I knew in Monmouth too, got word this week that her dad had died. It was a terrible shock as naturally it would be, but the worst thing about it was the fact that she is sitting around here doing nothing and she could have been home.

Just this minute I got the letter from Midge so I will cut this short so I can write to her. I got Dad's letter also in the same mail which I read first and when he said Midge had been sick and that you had talked with them on the phone I was a bit worried so I tore her letter open in a hurry. She told me all about it and having received an 8 page letter from me the day she had the D&C, which Dave read to her that evening. As long as I couldn't have been there, I'm glad my letter came to cheer her up. Guess if I'd been there I would have been mighty scared. Dave certainly is a wonderful husband. She's always singing his praises.

Also, I think an awful lot of Roy, more than I want to admit—but you just can't take things seriously over here. Situations and everything are so different over here. I do know that I have nothing to worry about concerning his engagement.

Also had a short note from Cookie. She says she sends her blessing to Roy and I, and she will loan me her black nightie after October 15th.

All my love,

Pill

MEMO

I well remember to this day, so clearly, that walk on the beach with Roy

He told me about his friend Friend (Col Friend). He always called him his "friend Friend" He said this friend was engaged to a girl back home and wanted to break his engagement and marry a nurse he had met on Tinian. He didn't know how to go about handling the situation.

I mulled it over in my mind., and said he should go to her when he gets stateside and maybe his true feelings will surface upon seeing her and talking with her and then perhaps he will be better able to do the right thing for both of them, for the three of them.

Then he admitted, as I had surmised, that he was talking about himself and not his friend Friend. Perhaps I should have been concerned but I wasn't worried, had no reason to be. I was secure in his feelings for me. He had proved it in every act and deed. You just know those things, in your heart and in your soul.

WED ON TINIAN
26 SEPT

Dearest Mom and Dad:

    Please excuse this brief note, but here I am again asking a favor of you. Could you get a card for Cookie and Bob and enclose $10 and also enclose my love. Wish I could be there but I just won't be able to, in fact this won't reach you before then, but she will get my card by the time they return home from the honeymoon. You are going to the wedding aren't you? Let me know all about it.

Love,

Pauline

LETTERS FROM TINIAN 1945

29 SEPT

SAT ON TINIAN

Dearest Mom and Dad:

Am enclosing some very poor candid shots. Roy and Ann took immediate possession of some of the best ones and I got stuck with these few. It's a 35mm camera. We are going to send the film away and have enlargements made, then you will be able to see them better.

Am busily reading an assignment that Roy gave me. "Traveler from Tokyo"—a concise picture of Japan as it was 1938-41.

We had some more immunization shots yesterday. Tonight 5 couples of us are going to a big dance at Roy's club "Dream Boat". You won't get mad if I tell you we always laugh when we hear of folks back home canning peaches. We have them so often, but I still like them.

What's Aunt Margaret doing in Delmar? Heard form Hazel a while back. She was still at Dix although she had been on the alert for ages. Remember Gladys Wright who went with Hazel and me? She had been to France and back and I believe is heading this way. Is she ever lucky. Wish I could have seen France.

Heard from Mrs. Ferguson again. She sounds very lonely and unhappy. It's about time I heard from Mr. Ferguson again.

You should see the bra top I made to wear around the house. I made it out of an air corps nylon map of the China coast. Two more maps and I can make a pair of shorts. You see quite a few map bathing suits on the beach and also parachute suits. You have to use anything here.

Floyd Smith is still in Missouri. Did I tell you he's a Sargeant now? Jim Goutremout is a civilian in Rochester now.

Roy and I are still hitting it off OK. When he gets stateside he says he's going to send me nylons, a cigarette lighter and a million and one other things. When he leaves he is going to give me his Parker 51 pen and pencil set with his name on it. He says for sentimental reasons.

Gotta write some more letters now and also get this in the mail stat.

Love an kisses

Be good,

Pill

LETTERS FROM TINIAN 1945

Dearest Mom and Dad:

We're still a'sittin' around here on Tinian. I'm really anxious to see Japan. As long as I'm over here I'd like to see a foreign country.

I suppose Cookie is having a wonderful time on her honeymoon. How I envy her. Wonder if I'll ever go on a honeymoon.

I've been spending most of my time this AM opening and closing my window. It's been raining on and off every few minutes all morning—in fact for the past few days.

Last night it was so chilly that I wore a T-shirt under my shirt and wore a necktie for the first time since leaving Honolulu. It was really comfortable. I was at the club coming from the "Pink and Blue" (powder room) to my table, when some boy who had had a little to drink spotted the tie and came up to me and said ties were not worn on Tinian and was trying to take it off me and Roy spotted him and you should have seen the fire in his eye. I got by without any trouble, the boy was only kidding but with Roy there, I had nothing to worry about. I'm his girl and he won't let anyone else come near me. He's a pretty wonderful guy—or have I told you that before?

Last night four of us went to a dark room on the field and developed about 6-8 rolls of film. It's very easy and I was quite pleased with my first job. I don't think I'd enjoy it for a daily job. I don't like it in the dark so long. Paper is very scarce here so we won't be able to print them. Roy thinks he'll send 'em to California to be printed so it will be quite some time before we see the finished product.

Gerry Grimm came over again Sunday and we played a few games of gin rummy.

Sunday night we went to see "Weekend at the Waldorf" but the theater was so jammed and people were even standing and it was pouring rain so we didn't stay. I was very disappointed because Van Johnson (sigh, sigh) was in it. It will be playing at various theaters on the island throughout the month so we should get to see it some time.

We have three dances scheduled so far this week—Weds, Thurs, and Sat., so we may go to the movies tonight if it doesn't rain too much. Thursday the 308th is throwing a farewell party because they are going to pack all equipment etc. the next day. It looks like we might be going sometime, but you know the army—you just have to sit and wait.

Last night it rained and blew and was really a rough night—and our jeep had no roof or windshield. My rain coat protected all of me except my face and it was all mud. My glasses were just solid mud and I couldn't see out of them. We have more fun though, with our problems. Anything to eliminate the boredom of sitting and waiting.

Doug Ferguson is at Great Lakes awaiting reassignment. Mrs. F. sounds very unhappy these days. I wonder what the score is re Doug's marriage. Maybe Mr. F. will write again and tell me. He's a funny guy. This is what Mrs. F said in her last letter: "It seems lonesome for the 3 of us, Mr. F., Doug and I at the table when I think of the time you were here—we were all happy then." Guess I'll have to write her a cheer up letter. I certainly never would have been happy if I'd married him. Did I tell you Doug has a mustache? Roy is growing one now. It's funny how people start growing them when they begin to get a little bald on top. It's time for Dave to start one.

One thing I really miss on the island is no store to go shopping in. Back home, if I really needed something all I had to do was go downtown and could usually find it. Every day I think of one thing or another that I need, but it's such a nuisance to have you go shopping for me and mail packages all the time. I'll start another list and then you can get it all at once. Another thing too, we have no idea what might be available in Japan and what we'll need there. Remember all that winter equipment and clothing I sent home? We are going to get another issue of it, if we do go to Japan. I wonder if I'll ever have to turn that in—some of it I'd like to keep.

That's about all for now.

Love,

Pill

P.S. Maybe you'll have to send my income tax refund here for me to sign—tell me how to endorse it too. I'm going to get a "Power of Attorney" soon so you can sign 'em for me and take care of other things that might arise.

8 OCTOBER 45

Dearest Mom and Dad:

Intended writing a long letter today while I was on OD duty but I was so busy I didn't get any of my personal things done.

Last night Roy and I celebrated our 2nd anniversary—2 months. Tomorrow we celebrate our 9th anniversary—9 weeks. I think that I can count the days on one hand that we have left together. No doubt we'll never meet again, but I have known happiness here on Tinian with him.

I have a date in 20 minutes and have to get dressed. Tomorrow I'll write a longer letter.

Love, Pill

P.S. Excuse scribble, I'm sitting on my bed with nothing to write on and writing on my lap.

LETTERS FROM TINIAN 1945

Dearest Mom and Dad:

Here is the long letter I promised you I'd write last night but I can't say how long it will be.

Received a nice long letter from Cousin Johnny L. in Alaska. What a snow job he gave me. He mentioned seeing a picture of me in the Albany paper—was that the one that was in about a year ago? He's anxious to get out of the army. He speaks of the nice cool Vermont hills. They fly a route from Anchorage to Seattle but he was on leave or something when Dan and Lyn were there so he missed them. I don't know if he had a chance to meet Lyn's family. He didn't mention it.

Heard again from Mrs. Ferguson. She writes quite frequently these days. She has been pretty upset this past year over Doug's marriage. She even went so far as to say that Doug hadn't wanted a baby till after he finished school, and that he was disappointed about it. It is a girl. Can't imagine Doug being a father.

About four or five days ago we had what I considered a hurricane. It rained and blew terrifically all night long and thru the next morning. None of us could sleep. I was afraid the quonset was going to blow away. I've never known such a strong wind before. I was afraid to go out to the latrine in the morning for fear I'd blow away. Finally two of the girls bundled up in their raincoats and hightops and ventured forth. They made it out and back safely so I figure if they could make it I could also. The latrine had moved off its moorings and shifted a foot northward, the roof was half gone and what remained was torn to shreds, so we had to sit in the wet and muddy latrine and gaze at the great outdoors. One side of our shower room was ripped and the handles were gone from some of the showers. Poor Roy and the other gears who live in tents. They were completely wet and many of the boys were without tents and had to sleep in the briefing room. We drove down to the area the evening after the storm and it really was a mess. Don't understand why the higher ranking officers live in tents while the others live in quonsets. That's enough of that. It was all very exciting and I'll chalk it up to experience.

At present I am reading "Black Boy" by Richard Wright, which I find quite interesting and easy reading. Am still waiting to read "Forever Amber" which there are several copies of here in our quarters.

We had shots in our arms again today. Looks like we really are going somewhere. All the married nurses and the girls with enough points received their orders to be transferred to one of the other units here on this island. They expect to go homeward soon. We have received girls from some of the other units to replace them.

No doubt it is all right for me to tell you a few things. There were five hospital units of nurses that came over on the ship with us and who are living right here with us and likewise doing nothing as we are. Apparently we are the lucky unit that has been selected to go on. What the other units will be doing I don't know but it looks as if one of them will be going stateside soon. I'd hate to think of going stateside again so soon. I want to see a little something while I'm over here.

Roy expects to leave for home in about two weeks and we no doubt will be leaving before that. I wonder if I'll ever see him again

Sunday we went around the island and took some more pictures. Last night we developed more films. It's fun. I wish we had some of the paper so that I could learn to print pictures. Guess it will be a long time before we will see any of the finished work. Roy gave me some rolls of film so that I can take lots of pictures in Japan. Of course we may never go to Japan. We never got to Europe. Better not tell any of this stuff to anyone until you do get word of our arrival. Things are still carried on with the same amount of secrecy although censorship is practically nil.

You will probably be mad when I tell you about the crap game I got into. All the clubs here have crap tables and every night you can see big games going on with $5, $10, and $20 bills being tossed all over the place. Sunday three of us couples were tired of taking pictures so we went to the club and played "Oh Hell" a simple card game, for a couple of hours and soon tired to that. The crap table was empty so the gang of us gathered around and were betting nickles and dimes and sometimes 3 cents. I didn't understand the fine points, but I started out with no money and ended up with $1.65. Don't worry about having to give me a lecture on gambling. I give one to the boys every night, when they leave our table to shoot five or ten or twenty. Sometimes they come back with nothing and sometimes with a hundred. Frankly I don't want to take the chance.

Haven't heard from Ramon since just before I left Fort Bragg. Wonder where he's going to school now. Smitty is still at Crowder and had nothing of interest to offer. Haven't heard from Jack Cassel in a few weeks so I don't know if he is still in Honolulu or on his way to Tinian or where.

The package still hasn't arrived, but it takes a long time for them to get here. I'm anxious mostly for the mascara. Don't remember what else I did ask for.

I can't think of anything else to say right now. I have to go to the PX and see what I can stock up on in case of no supplies in Japan. The way I talk you'd think I was really going.

Haven't heard from Cookie lately. No doubt she is having a wonderful time. Be good and have some fun.

Love, Pill

P.S. One of the older women in our unit who is going home, spends about every other weekend in Delmar (used to, I mean). She might call you up. Her name will be Mrs. Ibbott I presume.

P.P.S : I ate with Roy in the "Gear Box" Sunday. Did I feel important. Waiter service and plates to eat off from.

Dearest Mom and Dad:

The package arrived safe and sound today, with the exception that the seeds were a bit loose in the box. Maybe I won't be able to do any planting until spring since the weather in Japan is about the same as it is stateside.

Just wrote a 5 page letter to Alta. She writes that Jimmie is having trouble in school with the teacher he has this year. He gets "9 o'clock fever" as Alta calls it.

Guess I told you I received a nice long letter from Capt. Lamson. Since he is or will soon be discharged, I guess I won't be able to answer it.

We went to the beach yesterday for the first time in almost 2 weeks. Since some of the men have already gone home from his group, Roy is getting new jobs every now and then. He is the group radar officer, S2 officer, historical, claims, investigating and RCM. All and all it keeps him busy. His CO, Colonel Jim, may leave in a few days and Roy is going to have to be the CO in charge of all the troops. Pretty important guy.

Roy just signed up for the Regular Army. He was recommended for a plan in which he will go to college, do research and also have some overseas work. If all goes well, he may get orders any minute to fly home and get started. Under regular army status, rank is much different than during the war. He may be a Capt. under those conditions.

Received another County Post today. There wasn't much news in that issue.

We are expected to get our orders any minute. Had our shipping number stenciled on our luggage yesterday. Maybe tomorrow.

Roy is always bringing me nice stories from the men in his outfit. Two other Majors told Roy I was the nicest girl that they had seen around there. Made me feel pretty good. These are older men. The club officer always comes over to our table and greets me with a big smile and dances with me. The other day Roy told Col. Jim that we wanted to announce our engagement (don't worry, he was only joking) at the club and the Col. said he wanted to give the bride away. The next time I saw him, he gave us his congratulations. There seem to be an awful lot of very nice men in that group. I certainly will miss the nice times we've had at the club "Dream Boat".

Guess I had better write to the State Department concerning my state registration.

I would like to make a request to have the "Town Talk" mailed to me over here if it is possible for me to get on their mailing list.

Referring to a clipping I received the other day, life here is not dull and women are not scarce—like Ralph Denman's speeding tickets.

Roy has given me some silver "rope" that I am going to use for Christmas decorations in Japan. I wonder if they have any celebration there for Christmas. Also, he gave me about a dozen rolls of white nylon ribbon which will come in very handy.

Your present to Cookie and Bob sounds very nice. I think an awful lot of her too. Sandra Smith is pretty young, isn't she? She must have looked pretty cute. I certainly wish I could have seen Jane. I bet she did look lovely.

Guess that's all for now. I'll keep writing so you'll know when you don't hear, that I'm on my way. Thank you for the package of the articles I requested. Now I have no excuse for failure to write.

Love, Pill

Lt. Denman A.N.C. TINIAN ISLAND 1945

LETTERS FROM TINIAN 1945

Dear Mom and Dad

We still have nothing new concerning leaving, but the rumors are flying thick and fast, pro and con.

Just got your letter today with the Christmas tags which I shall use. Also am glad you got the shoes. No telling when they'll arrive. It certainly takes a long time for packages.

Have been busy reading "Forever Amber" and when someone else has the book I read some Ellery Queen stories. We have loads of reading material here. We have the overseas editions of most all magazines.

Now that Roy has so many new jobs, I find myself with more time, but I'm certainly getting lazy. I lie around on my sack, reading most of the time. He just called me up on the phone to say he couldn't get a jeep this PM but will be over without fail at 6:30. We haven't missed an evening yet, but we do come in as early as 9 PM now and then. They say this island is about 40 square miles. It's not very large. You can go all around the island in very little time.

Roy is engaged, but I'm very sure that he is not intending to marry her and if he does it is apt to be from obligation. I somehow don't think he'll ever marry. He's so much like I am. Always having deep infatuations, but they soon fade out as another comes along. We both have admitted that to each other, and although we have even mentioned marriage, neither of us are serious. No doubt by the time I get stateside, we'll each have found someone else, and if not, it will be time enough then to be thinking seriously of anything.

Don't ever worry about me getting married on the spur of the moment. I would never be so foolish. I'm too scared of marriage I guess.

I have so many letters to write but just can't get around to writing any. I'm really getting lazy I guess.

We finally got to the show and saw "Weekend at the Waldorf"—Van Johnson and Xavier Cugat. The picture was good but Van wasn't in it half enough. I was very disappointed.

I was in the sun at the beach for 2 hours yesterday and I didn't change in color one little bit.

We had a group picture taken of all the girls in our unit, and it came out terrible. It is out of focus and pretty bad all around.

The girls who left our unit went to Saipan Saturday and expect to leave for home today.

Did I tell you I'm getting a wisdom tooth? It's causing no trouble except I keep poking at it with my tongue.

I can understand your point re Aunt Margaret. I think it is difficult when relatives live together no matter how fond you are of them. I know that I would feel uncomfortable if anyone else lived in our house.

I think Midge and Dave should come to see me on their second week of vacation. After all, you have seen them and it's my turn now. Hope Midge is feeling okay now.

This was supposed to be a short note but when I write to you I can just amble on and on. Guess that's all.

How are or were the grapes this year?

Flash! Latest rumor—leaving in 48 hours. Just a rumor—maybe 48 days—who knows?

Be good and thanks for shopping for me.

Love, Pill.

18 OCT '45

Dearest Mom & Dad,

Just a hurried note. Am in the middle of a mess of packing. I have 23 hours before my luggage gets picked up.

Last nite Roy and I were here at the movies and when we returned to our jeep, it was gone. Someone stole it and we're pretty worried. $900 is nothing to sneeze at. Time will tell.

Gotta get back to my packing now so I can get shaped up for my last (maybe) date with Roy.

Am enclosing another souvenir for the scrap book. It was from the trip over.

Love,

Pill

We were all loaded onto the trucks and went by convoy to the Tinian Harbor where our transport awaited to take us to Japan (?) to take part in the occupation of Japan.,(?) Roy and Schrank followed us in a jeep to see us off. A lot of tears were shed, and bear hugs passed around and many good bye kisses were wet with the tears of parting. Roy gave me his prized gold Parker 51 pen and pencil set, on which his name was engraved. He told me to practice writing, "MRS" in front of that name with the pen. I promised him I would do that with pleasure. He will stay on the island commanding the remaining troops before going stateside and I will be off in Japan working in the 308th General Hospital. Parting is never easy, but this was especially hard—we had had so little time and had so much more to share, and see and do, and it was too soon to be separated. Japan was so far from Uncle Sugar Able, and we knew not how long we would be with the occupation.

> When we two parted
> In silence and tears,
> Half broken-hearted
> To serve for years
> Pale grew thy cheek and cold
> Colder thy kiss.
> Byron, "When We Two Parted"

LETTERS FROM TINIAN 1945

Dearest Mom and Dad,

Here we are on our way again—where? No one told us but it's no doubt Japan. I surely hate leaving Roy after ten weeks of seeing him twice or three times daily. The night before we left I got all sharped up in my new beige skirt, white starched shirt and maroon neck tie and was Roy proud of me. Kacki (?) and o. d. gets pretty tiresome after a while. Yesterday Roy (and his pal Schrank who goes with my friend Maxine) followed our truck convoy down to the docks and kissed us good bye before we went on board. Isn't it silly for a man to kiss a girl good bye and have her sail away and he wait on the dock? That's the result of war.

He gave me his Parker 51 pen and pencil set for sentimental reasons and told me to practice writing "Mrs. Roy Oscar Spencer with it. Wonder when and if I'll see him again. Wonder if it is same as any other infatuation. He's pretty busy now since Colonel Jim left. He is now in charge of a few thousand men. He still has time to feel lonesome. When he met me at the dock he said that he was lonesome already. It's going to get more and more lonesome for him because all his buddies that have been with him since the days in India are leaving, a few planes leaving for the states each evening.

I heard something pretty nice about Roy today. His C. O., Col Jim, thinks he's a near genius, and the best radar man he's known.

Well that's enough of that chatter. We are in Saipan harbor now and it sure is exasperating to be sitting here in the harbor doing nothing, but gazing over at Tinian. It's morning now and we've been sitting here since before supper last evening.

This ship isn't as nice as the Matsonia and yet it has many more advantages. We all live in one big dorm, crowded but at least it is cool and there are doors opening from our room onto the deck. We have triple deckers and I have a lower this time. We have hot water for the first time since leaving the states in July. Had a hot shower and shampoo this morning. And yet there is nothing like a cold shower in hot weather. We eat in style amid the naval officers. We have life belts rather than life jackets, which is a wonderful improvement. Last night we went to a movie on board (top side); it was cool and it didn't rain. We saw "Thunderhead, Son of Flicka". The scenery was really beautiful.

I'm still reading "Forever Amber", then I'll read "Captain from Castile" and then the "Green Dolphin Street". We've been playing bridge again, so I may not even finish the first one. Also I have a book on the Japanese language which I may study from time to time

Rumors say we'll only stay in Japan until March. Other rumors say that we won't even stay in Japan,—that cancellation of our orders to go there are already on their way. We just live on rumors in the army. Once we get started it should take only a few days to get to Japan.

I better close now and get some other letters answered. Haven't written to Midge for a while, nor Jane & Elsie. Can't wait to hear from Cookie. She's pretty busy no doubt.

That's all for now.

Love and kisses,

Pill

To meet, to know, to love-and then to part
Is the sad tale of many a human heart.
Samuel Taylor Coleridge (1772-1834)

RESTRICTED
HEADQUARTERS 468 BOMBARDMENT GROUP
APO 183

21 October 1945

GENERAL ORDERS
NUMBER 33

Under the provisions of paragraph 4, AR 600-20, and pursuant paragraph 1, Special Orders 139, Headquarters 58th Bomb Wing, 12 October 1945, the undersigned hear by assumed command of the Ground Echelon, 468 Bombardment Group (VH) during the temporary absence of Colonel James V. Edmondson 022573, United States Army

ROY OSCAR SPENCER
Major, Air Corps
Commanding

RESTRICTED

21 OCTOBER 1945
TINIAN HARBOR

Dear Mom and Dad,

We didn't get very far on our voyage. We went to Saipan, fuelled, came back to Tinian and here we sit loading equipment. Tomorrow, maybe, the other unit of nurses will come aboard. Three days wasted and no shore leave and still in Tinian. What a set up.

Went on a conducted tour of the ship this P. M. Talked with the navigator and he showed me the proposed course of this ship. Non stop to Kure, if ever we leave here.

Having good meals. Steak, French fries and ice cream tonight. Cold cuts and potato salad this noon. First potato salad since the last voyage.

Heard from Hazel. She's still at Dix and fed up with the set up. She ran into Jane and Bob shortly before their marriage.

This letter should be mailed on Tinian tomorrow. I'd love a copy of the Delmar Town Talk if there are any available.

This trip our officers, enlisted men and equipment are all on board with us.

Did you say Ruth Hafley had a baby? I didn't know she had finished training, although I do remember of her marriage.

This letter is rather dull but I'm all ready to hit the sack and am a bit sleepy. I retired at 8:30 last eve but I eat at 6 A.M. so I have to sleep early.

Be good and don't worry.

Love,

Pill

LETTERS FROM TINIAN 1945

POEM

When the bright sunlight simmers

Across the sea so blue

When the clear fountain in the

Moonlight glimmers

I think of you

I am with you wherever you are

Roaming

And you are near!

The sun goes down and soon the

Stars are coming

How I wish that you were really here

GOETHE

JAPAN

FRIDAY—NEAR JAPAN
26 OCTOBER 1945

Dearest Mom and Dad,

Here we are in the channel approaching Kure—and is it ever cold. It was a nice long summer. I hate to see winter come, I don't have enough adipose tissue to keep me warm. This looks like mountainous country and our sleeping bags will be very welcome since the rumor is that our home will be tents.

We pulled out of Saipan Monday eve about 10:30. It was very lonely spending all day Sunday on board in Tinian Harbor. They took us on a tour of the ship to break up the monotony.

The trip was uneventful with the exception of pretty rough water yesterday. Made me feel kinda funny inside. Spent most of the time in my sack reading. Finished "Forever Amber", read a murder novel and I'm now reading, "A Tree Grows in Brooklyn". I borrowed the latter from the ship's library and doubt if I'll finish it before we leave. We've been playing some cards too.

The meals have been very good——we've had steak twice, and ice cream quite frequently. This cool weather is giving me a better appetite.

I'm going to take some pictures of this land to go in the scrap book. Roy gave me some rolls of film and I'll borrow a camera to take the pictures.

I've been going to bed awfully early since I got on board. There isn't much room to sit around here. We use the mess hall when meals aren't being served and there isn't room for many of us there.

Now that I've seen Japan, I'm content to go back to Tinian or stateside.

This isn't much of a letter, but there isn't much to write.

Heard from Doug Ferguson. He is out here in the Pacific somewhere again. Also had another long letter from his dad. Heard from Ramon. He is in business in Troy, saving up enough money to go home. He says he gets lonesome too.

Can't wait to land and start getting mail again. Wonder if Roy misses me. When he saw me off last Friday he said he missed me already. Guess he likes me a little.

Bye for now. Gotta go and see how the scenery looks now.

Love and kisses,

Pill

NURSES ARRIVING IN KURE. JAPAN

OCTOBER, 1945

Upon our arrival on land we were immediately greeted by a group of American soldiers saying, "Ohio, Ohio" (Japenese for hello) and producing this sign. I quickly whipped out my lipstick and crossed off "NO WOMEN".

31 OCTOBER 1945
KURE, JAPAN

Dear Mom and Dad,

Just a note to let you know that we arrived safe and sound. We are working and finding time to play too.

This is quite a country. I started a long letter to you today which I shall finish tomorrow but am dropping a quick note just in case some mail should go out tomorrow.

Doubt if mail service will ever be good. It's 11:30 PM. Gotta hit the sack so I can work tomorrow.

Love and kisses,

Letter follows,

Pill

KURE, JAPAN 31 OCTOBER 1945
HALLOWEEN
ON DUTY (DON'T FAINT)

Dear Mom and Dad:

Guess I haven't written since we got off the ship. Sunday we received orders for half of us to leave the 308th on detached service. Twenty-three of us are here with the 361st station hospital in Kure. About twenty others went to a field hospital in Hiro.

This hospital has been in operation about three weeks and without any nurses until our arrival.

The nurses who are attached to this hospital are on their way over—when and if they arrive is a question. We are pinch hitting until their arrival. The rest stayed with our unit and are now setting up the hospital in the "Annapolis of Japan", on an island near Kure. We hated breaking up but we are all only a few miles apart and we'll rejoin our unit sometime.

I'm on an eight hour daily shift, on a medical floor—all I do is take temps and pass out medicine and it takes all day to do that. We are busy getting this business organized. It needs a nurses' touch. We have eighty or so patients on our ward but no one is very sick. I think the boys heard of our arrival because we keep getting more patients.

There is so much to tell and it's so difficult to describe things as they are. We went sightseeing in a jeep on my off duty time this afternoon. The Japs stare at us as much as we stare at them. We're the first white women they've seen, and a blonde is something very unusual. I wish I had a camera with me. We see everything that is typically Japanese.

Their clothing, buildings, etc., women with their babies on their backs, wearing kimonos.

Most everyone wears clogs, holding the strap with their big toe.

PAULINE D. WEBB, (LT. PAULINE A. DENMAN, A. N. C. WWII)

Didn't get much written. We've been quite rushed the last few days, so much so that we are putting beds in the hall. We had twenty admissions in one day and it really kept us busy.

A lot of the colored boys have been drinking some bootleg liquor sold by the Japs which is made of menthol alcohol, I believe. We have had several of them come in—two of them died within a few hours. It was rather disgusting, especially since there have been previous deaths from the same cause and the boys have been warned, but some of them just don't believe it. We are getting in a lot of venereal disease which was apparently picked up on Luzon.

It burns me up to have to take of patients like these, not that there is much to do for them, but it keeps us so busy and so filled up with desk work, etc.

Oh well, that's how the work is here. We don't mind too much, it's just that it's so unnecessary.

The first evening here three of us went out with our acting chief nurse as the guest of a colonel who lives a few doors away. We had a very nice evening, chatting and eating, etc.

He lives in a real Japanese home, (former residents were Japanese naval officers) with three other colonels. It's a beautiful Jap house with a special tea room with mat floor and low table, a tree growing in the tea room, sliding paper and glass doors, etc. Before the evening was over eight full colonels and one Lt. Colonel were doing their best to entertain us. It was all very interesting but not for more than one evening. They were all regular Army West Pointers and old enough to be uncles.

The next night we went to an officer's club which is in a former restaurant. We had to take our shoes off before entering and leave them in the doorway. The room was furnished with six to eight tables about a foot high, and pillows for everyone to sit on. We had Japanese waitresses who were very entertaining. They had beer, tea and pretzels and talked (sign language) with us. The boys have taught them to sing "Auld Lang Sine". "Suwanne River", "Red Wing" etc. They taught the tune to them but not the words except one or two. They understand "thank you" and answer back "you're welcome". You spend the entire evening just watching them and "talking". There are two Jap boys there who act as interpreters so we can find out various things of interest. The girls were very much amazed at seeing my blonde hair. The girls wear beautiful kimonos with some fancy thing around the waist that is very compli- cated to put on. One of the girls demonstrated and it is quite a process. It is so cool that I always bring an extra pair of woolen socks and wear my G. I. long underwear. We've been going to that club every night and playing bridge and "oh hell". Curfew rings at twelve two nights a week, and at eleven the rest of the week. Rules about escorts are the same as on Tinian.

Hiroshima is about one and a half hours from here by jeep, but it is off limits for us much to our dislike. I'd like very much to actually see the atomic bomb destruction.

Kure is pretty well bombed out and the roads are terrible. We drive on the left side of the street.

When we arrived at the dock a lot of little Japanese boys about ten years old carried our heavy suitcases for us. There was a crude sign at the dock. "Welcome to Kure, no wine, no women, no fraternization, no bartering, no city". I took my lipstick and crossed out the "no" in front of "women". One of the kids took a picture of that which I hope someday to have a copy. I certainly wish I had Roy's 35 mm camera with me so I could take a lot of pictures of the people and the damage and the homes.

We live in a two story wooden building with steam heat and running (cold) water with single rooms and double rooms. We have cots with mattresses, a dresser, bedside table and small chair. I've put some maps and Varga girls etc on the wall so the room doesn't look too badly. The only way we get warm water is to fill our helmets and put them on the radiator.

Our showers are ice cold and thus I've taken none. All I've done is take sponge baths out of my helmet and the water is warm only in the eve.

Our "john" is terrible. The Japs call it the "bengie"—it is porcelain or enamel with flush but it is sunk into the floor and you have to squat to go and its a problem. It is a modified "slit trench". Today they built a wooden seat over it so it is like a regular latrine and "heavenly".

What a relief.

I exchanged $10.00 into yen today and got squared away as to the Jap money system.

Fifteen yen to a dollar, one hundred sen to a yen. I'll enclose some for you to keep for curiosity if nothing else. The hundred yen bill is almost as big as two of our U. S. Bills.

We don't use change at all. One of the bills is about three cents.

Everyone tries to get souvenirs and cigarettes and soap and gum and candy are good bar- tering items, although you are not supposed to barter. My date brought me a little Jap doll last night. Some people are crazy and buy kimonas for one thousand yen. Of course most people keep to themselves as to where they got their souvenirs and what they cost in money or barter. I'd like to get a fan and a pair of those clogs.

Tonight I am going on a blind date to a party. I'd rather stay in but I promised to go. Tomorrow I am going to a sookie-achi dinner (excuse spelling).

The boy Bob E. I have been going out with is a first lieutenant and a perfect gentleman, married, has a mustache, very nice looking, a marvelous dancer, but I'll take Roy any day. He's 28 and expects to go home shortly. Most of the troops that are here came from Mindanou and Luzon and there abouts.

We haven't gotten any mail at all since we left Tinian. My radio is working very nicely. I have it in one of the other girl's room because my outlet doesn't work. We get good music on it.

PAULINE D. WEBB, (LT. PAULINE A. DENMAN, A. N. C. WWII)

One time on Tinian the radio was tuned into the Hit Parade and the first three songs were unfamiliar to all of us. Makes me feel like I've been away from the states for a long time.

The patients all laugh when I tell them I have been overseas three months. Most of them have been over two to three years and are all yellow from having taken atabrine.

Heard today that the 308th goes into operation the 11th of this month, but I presume we'll stay here until the 361st nurses arrive. Rumor has it that they have just arrived in Tokyo. I rather hate going to the 308th because curfew is at 6 PM and there is no place at all to go, or nothing to do.

We have about eight to ten Japanese girls working in our barracks (home) and are to do anything we ask. They make our beds and clean our rooms daily, do washing and ironing for us. One is an American born girl who lived in California until she came here four years ago so she speaks English and Japanese and we get our work done by talking to her.

This letter is awfully long and no doubt boring. Maybe I will have to supplement some pictures sometime soon. Maybe you could send it along to Midge and Dave so I won't have to rewrite it to them.

I've written this in a hurry because I just haven't had time to do anything but unpack and go out. We are afraid we might go back to 308th soon and there won't be anything to do over there except write letters.

Love and kisses,
Happy Thanksgiving,

Pill

11 NOVEMBER 1945

Dearest Mom and Dad,

Nothing new or exciting around here. Except we will go over to the 308th very soon. The footlockers and bedding rolls of the new nurses arrived the other day so they can't be very far away themselves. The great 308th is finally in operation, amazing as it may seem. We evacuated a patient there yesterday.

I borrowed a camera and am going to take some pictures today if I can get a ride around the place. Today is my day off so I have all day in which to do it. Bob may have to work but if he doesn't he's going to take me around to snap a few pictures.

Two days ago we finally got some mail. I heard from Alta, Aunt Margaret, Cookie and you. They were mailed October 23, 24 and 25. No mail has come through from Tinian yet. I'm pretty anxious to hear from a certain party who may or may not still be there.

I had a can of Japanese tangerines for breakfast this morning and it was very good. I'm listening to my radio now in the room across the hall. Two Jap women are doing some ironing in here and chatting away.

I plan to stay in the Army only as long as necessary. By the time they get around to release me I'll be more than willing to accept a discharge. Now that the war is over, and I have seen Japan, I'd be willing to go home any day. It's time I settled down and started my own family. I'm getting old. Almost 25.

I didn't happen to know Chaplain Metzger but perhaps Roy did since he belonged to the same unit—the 58th Bombardment Wing, pioneering B-29 unit, etc. I will ask him. Wouldn't it have been funny if Roy and I had gotten married on Tinian and had him perform the ceremonies.

It is 10:30 in the morning and Sammy Kaye is on the radio now. A year ago today at 11 A.M. on Armistice Day we were in basic learning how to put on a gas mask. I'm still carrying the old gas mask but don't know why. We haven't had the authority to throw them away.

I haven't written many letters yet from Japan. I better write to Cookie soon. I've been making some Christmas cards. Think I'll go to the market and sell them for a yen apiece. I'll make a million.

Gotta close now. Love and kisses and Happy Thanksgiving.

Pill

P.S. Could you send me a couple of books of airmail stamps in your next letter.

LETTERS FROM TINIAN 1945

15 NOVEMBER 1945
KURE, JAPAN

Dearest Mom and Dad,

We are still here, but expecting to go over to the 308th any time. I've finally rationed myself to two dates a week so I can get some rest and some work done. Makes the boys mad but I just can't work and keep up the routine of Tinian Times.

The mail finally came through—to the extent of thirty letters this week—about ten from you and fourteen from Major Roy. He has been writing about twice a day, but I can't say the same for me. Tomorrow I'll sit down and answer all your letters and any questions you might have asked. Roy is scheduled to leave Tinian today. Wonder what will happen when he returns to Uncle Sugar Able and sees Kathrine again. Time alone can tell.

I promise to write tomorrow.

Love and kisses, Pill

P.S. Could you call up Mr. Abell concerning my new APO. I just haven't been able to get any letters written.

Love, P. Spencer

SUNDAY 18 NOVEMBER 1945
KURE
FREEZING

Dearest Mom and Dad,

Am going through your letters now to answer any of your inquires. Do you think you could possibly buy presents for Midge and Dave, also Elsie and Jane. I have no place here at all to buy anything. The only store for miles around is our small PX which has nothing to offer but toilet articles and very little of them. Around $3-5 each for Midge and Dave; around $3.00 each for Elsie and Cookie. I hate to have you doing all these things for me, especially what I am going to ask you now. Do you think you could buy something for Roy for me? I'll have to give you the address later, maybe not until after Christmas. How about getting him the best looking wallet that Albany has to offer and having his name put on: "ROY O. SPENCER". Also about a dozen hankies and some shorts (loud and striped), large size, maybe three pair. Maybe later I will think of something else. He's been pretty wonderful to me and there is so little that I can do for him.

Fresh flowers are still blooming here and the Jap girls keep bouquets in our rooms constantly.

Enjoyed the pages from the Town Talk. Next month they can include a picture of me behind bars, in Japan, unable to come home for a while. That's the way it seems. It's so cold everywhere, no hot water except on rare occasions. No place to go and nothing of any beauty to see, except ruins and destruction, and the stench is awful. Winter is bad enough anyway without having to be cold. Maybe things will be different on Eta Jima where the great 308th is located. We may go over there soon. Today a gang of male officers arrived here. Maybe the girls will arrive some day.

Things really aren't bad here. It's just that I'm in a bad mood today. "Putchakins" you always called it. It's just that I want to go home and marry Roy before it is too late.

Could you also include in his (Roy's) gifts some men's stationary with "Roy O. Spencer, Major Air Corps" on it. Don't worry if these things won't be able to be ready before spring. I may not have a stateside address of his for a while, and if he gets married, they'd make good wedding presents.

Maybe I'm conceited, but if he marries Maggie, he'll be sorry, just as were Hudson & Doug. Boy am I crazy!!

How do you like my new writing? It's the way Roy writes and I'm learning to forge his letters.

Your idea for seat covers sounds very nice. Clever girl. I'll let you know immediately when my shoes arrive or any of the other packages arrive.

Right now I'm listening to my radio in the room across the hall from my room. I have on a sweater and field jacket over my uniform

I mailed the clippings re the chaplain to Roy, since he might know him.

Selling the twin beds sounds like an excellent idea. A double bed or a couch would make a nice cheerful room. I just won't know the place when I see it.

I still haven't seen the September 24 issue of Life yet. I hope Jimmie Stewart won't be hurt if I marry Roy.

Guess I've written enough for one sitting. I'll try to write more often even though there probably won't be much to report.

The radio programs here aren't too bad. There is one Jap station which I never listen to naturally; but there is a local Kure station with all American programs. Mostly rebroadcasting of the usual evening programs, minus the commercials. Right now the Army-Wisconsin game is going on.

That's all for now.

Love, Pill

P.S. Next time you send a package, I could use some writing paper.

P.P.S. The enclosed is something I received from Roy recently. You can mail it back to me some day.

DAY BEFORE THANKSGIVING 1945

Dear Mom and Dad,

Just a note. Things are about the same. We are awfully busy and very badly in need of help. Received a 7 November letter from you today. I think I received later postmarks than that a couple of days ago.

Here is Roy's address for Christmas packages:

> Maj. Roy O. Spencer 0-439809
> 349 West 95th Street
> Los Angeles, Calif
> % Mrs. Frank Hepburn

Heard from Lt. Jack Cassell (Ft. Bragg date) again yesterday. He arrived on Tinian after I left and hunted all over for me. Then he flew to Japan and went everywhere in Tokyo trying to find out the location of the 308th but without success. He returned to Guam and is now headed back to Honolulu. Was he ever disgusted. He was a nice guy but too, too handsome.

Heard from Mrs. Ferguson again today. She had been visiting in Michigan and had a nice time.

Not much else to write. Happy Thanksgiving tomorrow.

Love, Pill

ETA JIMA
28 NOVEMBER '45

Dearest Mom and Dad,

We came over here yesterday. It is a very beautiful place and I shall try to take some pictures sometime. The hospital buildings are all modern marble and quite magnificent. The girls that came here first (the ones who didn't go on detached service) have the choosiest living quarters. Rooms with fireplaces, thick rugs, drapes, bedspreads, etc. We have a nice Jap house but no heat; sliding doors and windows, mat floors, etc. Very clean and new. Not much closet space in our room. We have a tennis court which I hope to use very soon.

Fatigues are worn on duty due to no heating. The landscaping is beautiful and it is very pleasant during the hours of sunshine.

Our colonel has his own home and is sending for his wife. I'd be happy if Roy were here. He should be back in the states by December 2. I wonder if he will break down and marry Maggie. He assures me he won't, but it may be a different story when they get together again.

I think I am going on the 4 PM to midnight shift for the month of December. You know how I feel about that shift. I might not mind too much since I can spend the mornings and afternoons on the lawn and in the sunshine. The evenings are too cold to do anything and there's nothing to do anyway.

Not much news for now.

Love and kisses, Pill

OUR HOSPITAL, THE 308th GENERAL WAS SET UP IN THE FORMER
JAPANESE NAVAL ACADEMY SHOWN HERE
THE ANNAPOLIS OF JAPAN

30 NOVEMBER '45

Dear Mom and Dad:

Here I am on duty (4 PM-midnight) with four patients. What a rest after having one-hundred twelve patients. It's nice to be able to give real nursing care for a change.

Received the very nice Thanksgiving card today. Had a Christmas and birthday card from the Fergusons today. Spent most of last evening making Christmas cards. I'll have to hurry and finish them so that I can mail them before the rush.

We've been attempting to heat our rooms with individual charcoal "stoves", (earthen pots with sand in them). It helps to take the chill off the room, but we still have to dress warmly. Today it rained so I didn't get outdoors. It's really nice out when the sun shines. Maybe I won't mind the evening shift since there is nothing to do in the evening and the best time of day is when I'm off duty.

There isn't a thing to write about. My four patients are fresh post ops. But it was minor surgery and they aren't in pain, just have a little nausea.

Did I tell you I've given up smoking again? It's been just about a month now—and Roy sent me a beautiful Ronson cigarette lighter. Even that won't induce me to start smoking. Not until I want to anyway.

The wind is howling outside and it sound like another cold night. They are treating us O. K. Most of the girls complain a lot, but I haven't been on the island long enough to know. I suppose it does get rather monotonous on this island after a while with nothing to do. We are rather isolated and have to have special permission to go to the mainland. I'd like to go home now and get married to Roy and have a dog, etc., but I'll try and be patient and hope that he breaks his engagement. That's selfish of me but I think he's a pretty wonderful guy, and I'm selfish enough to want him. In a couple more days he will be docking in Frisco. Don't know how soon he'll be going to Detroit to see Maggie. If he comes to New York he's going up to Delmar to visit his "in-laws" as he puts it.

That's enough about Roy. There's nothing new about me. I like the food better here and my appetite is improving.

Did I tell you roses are still in bloom? The climate is warmer than at home this time of year, but due to no heating it seems so cold. We wear woolen underwear all day; fatigues on duty and off and look like a bunch of tramps most of the time. Comfortable and no need for girdles and silk hose at present.

I'll let you know as soon as packages start arriving. Yesterday I went hunting around and found some lumber and made a book case for our room. My room mate made some drapes for one end of the room which helps warm up the room a little. We try anything and everything to keep warm. I'm mighty glad I have my flannel robe and pajamas.

Gotta close now and write some more letters.

Love, Pill

LETTERS FROM TINIAN 1945

3 DECEMBER '45

ETA JIMA

Dear Mom and Dad:

Such a place this is. Our colonel, C.O. is leaving and the colonel from the 361st is taking over. Maybe he'll see that we get some heat. At the present time I have on my fatigues, woolen socks, T shirt, 100% wool dress shirt and field jacket. My fanny is cold but otherwise I am fairly comfortable. I have my charcoal burner going.

Thanksgiving day there was an explosion in one of the caves near here and it rocked the place, in fact we felt the jolt of it over in Kure. There was some picric acid in the caves that caused the explosion. So yesterday they decided to dynamite the cave to avoid any disaster. They evacuated all the patients, nurses, Japs and everyone from the hospital area. Those who were well hiked, and the rest rode via truck, ambulance and jeep to a safe area about two miles from here. We all built bonfires and sat around and had a fairly cool time. We ate rations and warmed them in the bonfire. One of the kids dropped a log on my little toe so I had to go home in the ambulance. Boy, was I lucky—didn't even have to go on duty yesterday or today. Took an X-ray and no fracture but my toe is purple so I hobble around in a bed room slipper.

Today we all had to evacuate the area again for two more blasts, and tomorrow it's said we go again. It's pretty tough on the night nurses because they work every night and have to spend the day evacuating and not getting much sleep. What a set up. Guess the 308th is always jinxed. I believe they are going to call this the 47th General Hospital soon and deactivate the 308th, but we nurses will stay on with the 47th General Hospital.

Heard from Alma Keefer today. She just had her appendix out and is recuperating very nicely.

I never did get to Hiroshima as much as I wish I could have. I presume I told you that we have to have special permission to take the ferry to the mainland. Last night all the girls were sitting around the little tent stove in the hallway griping about the whole situation. Most of the girls are very discontented here. I don't mind it as much as I did in Kure. The others would much prefer to be on the mainland. Maybe I'll change my tune after a while. I have no desire to go out, not even to the movies. I write to Roy every day and he writes once or twice a day. I presume now that he is stateside he'll do differently. Time will tell.

So you went to the movies. How about going to the movies here tomorrow night; it's Abbott and Costello. Did you notice in the "Affairs of Susan" that the man on the island put a pot under George Brent's bed?

Received an awfully nice Christmas card from Roy a couple of weeks ago. I will quote the verse and the corrections or changes he made in the verse:

Christmas greetings to a dear sister. (*nurse*)

Just to wish you happiness

And joy and pleasure, sis *(And fun and pleasure and joy)*
With lots of love and there can be
No better time than this *(.No better man than Roy)*

He's crazy. Didn't I tell you he was a character after we had our first date? But I'm crazy too, and a character. That explains our attraction.

Enough of this chatter. I have a picture of Roy's Maggie. She's 27, a brunette and very attractive. I'm worried.

Merry Christmas. Love, Pauline

P. S.: Can you put the enclosed on Roy's presents? How are you making out with all this extra Christmas shopping? Hope it isn't too much.

8 DECEMBER 1945

Dearest Mom and Dad:

Just a brief note. Life is going on as usual with nothing new at all to report, still working 4-12. Heard from Mrs. Ferguson and Doug is somewhere in Japan too. We may meet sometime soon. Small world.

Am awaiting word of Roy's safe arrival in U.S. of A. on December 2 or 3. No packages have arrived yet, but will let you know as soon as they do. Hope you don't have to spend the holidays alone. Next year we'll all be together.

The enclosed card shows a very small portion of this hospital. Our quarters are to the left and in the rear of the hospital on the side of the hill. Don't throw the card away because it is the only one I have. You could perhaps put it in the scrapbook if there's any room left. The Seasons Greetings card is for Aunt Ella. I don't know her name or address but she always remembers me. Could you forward it to her?

Isn't this paper beautiful? I'm on duty and have no paper here. Could you send me a few airmail stamps or books of stamps in letters now and then. They're so hard to get around here.

Hope you aren't going blind trying to read this. I had to write a letter for a patient tonight because he has eye trouble. It was to his wife and his name is Roy.

That's all for now, Love, Pill

Editors note: this letter was written on a Rx pad.

12 DECEMBER
ETA JIMA

Dearest Mom and Dad:

Just a hurried note as always. Yesterday packages started coming in. I received two from Rochester. Yours may be in the next shipment. The post office department is pretty over taxed. They were set up to service 10,000 troops but they are handling 40,000. They can't handle money orders or packages for the present. If you could send me a few books of three cent stamps and one cent stamps I'd appreciate it muchly. I received the two books the other day and really appreciated them because I didn't want to send all of my Christmas cards free lest they arrive next summer.

We were paid yesterday for the first time since leaving Tinian. The Jap money looks like a couple thousand dollars instead of just a hundred. I'm risking sending the enclosed $20.00 because I have too much yen and can't send money orders. Such a problem.

Received a nice hanky in the mail for my birthday from Margaret. Soon, in less than a week I should start receiving mail from Roy. I wonder how he enjoys it stateside.

Yesterday a lot of the kids got packages and opened their gifts. One of the girls got a bubble blowing (see Life October 15) set and we all were blowing bubbles all over the place. Just like Christmas morning—but what will they do on Christmas morning?

If the twenty dollars arrives safely, use it as a "working capitol" for all the little things I ask for. It should last about a week at the rate I go. I don't spend much money here except for writing paper and fruit juice. I'm still keeping my no smoking pledge. It's been about six weeks.

I'm still on the four to midnight shift and don't mind it at all. I sleep pretty cold, use my hot water bottle every night.

Gotta close now and go to chow. Not much of a letter. I'll let you know when the package arrives.

Love and kisses.

Pill

Happy New Year

17 DECEMBER 1945
ETA JIMA, JAPAN

Dearest Mom and Dad.,

One week from tonight is Christmas Eve. I surely hope you have some guests for Christmas. I promise I'll be there next year. I know I'll be stateside by then and as soon as I'm in the states I'm eligible for discharge. I suppose you saw the new order concerning eligibility for discharge

I'm still on 4-12. Expect to go off the 30th. I don't mind this shift at all. Saturday I went to the mainland (Kure) with some of the girls. Went to the quartermaster and the post office. Was able to get stamps, but don't worry if you've already sent some. They won't go to waste I assure you.

No more packages have arrived at the post office but there is still a week.

Last night, my evening off, I went to a party in Hiro but didn't have a very interesting time. The club had a big fireplace and Christmas tree all decorated and lit up. We went over to the mainland in the General's gig. Classy! The evening wasn't wasted tho, my date (Herman) gave me two rolls of 620 film. I took two rolls of film up the past week or two and am going to see about getting them developed soon. Went roaming in the hills the other day and got lots of shots of people and scenery.

Today they delivered electric heaters, one to each room. Now the electricians are busy wiring the house for use of the heaters. Won't be long now. We have a hot shower now which is a welcome thing. It works pretty well.

Heard from Elsie this week. Mel is busy these days training new men.

Expect to hear from Roy any day now. If the ship arrived on schedule, he's been in the states two weeks. Did I tell you Col. Matheson might drop in to say hello. He's the patient that I had in Kure. Also Roy will drop in when and if he comes east. That is if he doesn't drop off in Detroit and get married.

Guess that's all the news for now.

Love,

Pauline

P.S. I don't know who the people were that Mrs. Ibbott visits—she told me but the name wasn't familiar to me. I don't know her maiden name.

The enclosed is part of a letter from Mr. Ferguson. Thought you'd be interested in the P. S.. Doug is in Japan somewhere.

I see you have some new stationary too. I shall be anxious to see the rooms with the pretty new paper and drapes.

PAULINE D. WEBB, (LT. PAULINE A. DENMAN, A. N. C. WWII)

Don't know if Roy will be going to M. I. T. or not. He wanted to go and start in the November class. There may be another class starting in the spring. I can tell you more about it when I hear from him. He was recommended for a special course but I believe he wasn't able to get his application in in time. He does expect to do some post graduate work while in the Army.

Happy Easter, Love, Pill

Portion of Ferguson letter: " By the way we just finished cleaning your room. Painted the wood work and I varnished the floor this morning. All nice and ready for you. Maybe Mrs. F. will tuck you in. Also wrote both of my kids to nite, you and Doug".

LETTERS FROM TINIAN 1945

20 DECEMBER 1945

ETA JIMA

Dear Mom and Dad,

No news, but a few rumors as always. Yesterday medical supply received instructions to issue no more equipment or goods and to pack to be ready to move in three weeks. If they go, we go too; also the British are moving in as occupation troops in January; the Russians in February. A few conflicting rumors state: 1) We go to China, 2) We go to Northern Japan, 3) We go to San Diego. Of course, the third one is highly erroneous. Probably something one of the girls started just to see how far it would go.

I come off evenings the 30th and start night duty. Such is life. Guess it doesn't make a lot of difference. I've made no plans for the holidays or anything.

Still haven't heard from Roy. Must be his ship was late in arriving stateside. Received a birthday card from the church yesterday. No more packages have arrived as yet.

So Dave is going to Harvard. I bet they hate leaving their nice apartment in Rochester, and they'll miss Alyce and Mac. If Roy should go to M. I. T., he might be somewhere near them.

We are having weekly medical lectures now. One hour a week. Went to the first one yesterday. It was quite interesting and it really seemed good to go to medical lectures again, as long as we don't have to participate, the doctors do the work.

Went into the village to a Jap photographer and had some foolish pictures taken—six for 15 yen. We were dressed in slacks and combat boots. Six of us girls went and had a nice walk. It's good to get out of the area for a few hours. A couple of Jap electricians just walked into my room and are jabbering away about the wiring for the heater. Maybe we'll have heat soon. It takes them long enough to get things done.

We have pretty good meals here. Fresh meat almost every day.

Sorry to hear you were sick, Dad. Glad you are better. Did you find my bed very comfortable? I have been well and no colds so far.

Guess that's all there is to report now. I have a few more letters I want to get off today. They've been piling up again.

Be good, Love,

Pauline

22 DECEMBER '45
ETA JIMA, JAPAN

Dearest Mom and Dad,

Five of our girls are leaving at noon tomorrow for the states—all eligible for discharge, through age or points. One is Ruth Coplon the Schenectady girl, so she'll call you up someday.

Had a new experience yesterday. Rode in a "duck"—one of those amphibious trucks. We rode along the highway to the water's edge, shifted a couple of levers and across the water we went.

Sunday we are going on a trip to the island of Mea Jima (that is the way it is pronounced but I don't know the spelling). It is a few miles from here and is supposed to be an island of shrines. They say it is a beautiful spot, so I'm taking the camera along. We are leaving around 9 A. M., taking some rations and returning in time for me to go to work at four.

Sometime when you write, could you tuck in some embroidery cotton. I borrowed some from one of the girls and I want to pay her back. I borrowed bright red, bright green and dark brown. Also I might be able to use some black. I'm getting quite domestic, embroidering.

We at last have heat in our rooms and it certainly is a welcome change. Of course the weather outside isn't as cold as it has been.

Received some September, October and November Albany County Posts. They came through my old A. P. O. 247. Mr Abell has my present A. P. O. now. Mail hasn't been coming through very well lately. Only a few receive mail each day. No more packages. Maybe soon. Not much more to write.

Love, Pauline

Picture of nurses taken on Miyajima, a small island near Hiroshima
where they had visited the Itsukushima Shrine. In the picture is a
traditional Japanese gate, a Torii commonly found at the entry to a
Shinto shrine, this one being a "floating" gate as it is in the water, or
mired in mud at low tide.

23 DECEMBER 1945
ETA JIMA, JAPAN

Dearest Mom and Dad:

This has got to be a quickie because my body guard will be here in fifteen minutes to take me on my hospital rounds. I have a new job as evening supervisor (sometimes pronounced snoopervisor) of the hospital. The other girl left yesterday for the states so I am taking her job over. Merely a temporary position since I am going on night duty the 31st of the month. It is a very dull job with nothing to do but make rounds, arrange time schedules, write reports and act dignified (who am I kidding).

Took a boat trip to Mea Jima today but there wasn't much to see. So little in fact that I took only two pictures. Ate a couple of delicious ham sandwiches and have been drinking water like mad ever since.

No snow yet although they predict a White Christmas for this area. The weather is too mild at present. It was a beautiful sunny day today. Had a letter from Mrs. Ferguson again today. She writes very frequently and I have a difficult time keeping up with her.

Every room or ward in this hospital has a beautifully decorated Christmas tree but the Chief Nurses Office is bare of any evidence of the season. So for lack of anything better to do I put a big Merry Christmas sign on the blackboard in here in colored chalk. Even that won't help to add any Christmas cheer to a few characters who work here.

Guess what each member of the unit received for Christmas from those higher up? One large bottle of saki and one of wine. The saki bottle is like a regular ginger ale bottle in shape but is about two or three times the size. Don't know what to do with the stuff. They say the wine is terrible and I never even cared for the taste of saki.

Still no mail from Roy but I am waiting patiently. I know how army transportation is and also the mail service.

Tomorrow is Christmas eve and I shall be thinking of you and wishing I could be there. Hope Net and Irving can make it O. K.

No more space and no more rumors, so I shall close now.

Love, Pauline

25 DECEMBER 1945
ETA JIMA

Dearest Mom and Dad,

Here it is Christmas Day at 2045 and I am at work (?)., in my office not minding the circumstances too much. I really think I enjoy working on these holiday evenings rather than going out on a date. The patients are much more interesting to talk to than a blind date.

Last evening I put in extra time as I made my rounds of the various wards and talked with all the patients so it was more fun for both of us. These boys over here really appreciate talking with white women after all those months overseas.

Tonight I put aside my slacks and am wearing my dress uniform because the boys get mighty tired of seeing women in trousers. I might as well wear my class A uniform because I don't do any nursing at all, just a glorified secretary, so I might as well look like one.

Last night after duty almost all of the girls living in our house were sitting around the stove and by the tree talking and chatting until 2:30 A.M. We have a really nice group of girls in our house and they are nice to talk with.

Woke up this morning when my night nurse room mate came off duty and opened my presents while still in bed. Midge's box arrived but no other. From Midge and Dave I received some Emeraude perfume, Apple Blossom cologne, fancy dry skin soap, "Dynamite" Revlon set of nail polish and lipstick. From Alyce and Mac, a pair of silk panties. Opened a birthday package from Midge and Dave which contained two or three pair of panties and some very pretty hankies. All of the gifts arrived in perfect condition. From my roommate I received a box of Bond Street Talc and a hankie with "Pill" on it in red embroidery.

There was no mail service here today but they say that a lot of packages came in so maybe tomorrow I will have some more gifts.

Tomorrow is my day off and I am going to the engineers again to celebrate my birthday. Frankie is a very nice guy, cute and married. I met him while I was at the 361st and while going with the nice W. O. who left for Lyte or somewhere a few days after I left for Eta Jima.

I had our main meal at 5PM today and it was very delicious. We had everything you could imagine plus deviled eggs and stuffed celery. It was an excellent Christmas dinner and everyone was well satisfied with the meal. I think we get excellent food here. No snow for Christmas and the weather isn't too cold.

Tonight must be Christmas eve at home. I'm hoping that Net and Irving are there with you. Too bad Midge and Dave couldn't make it. Maybe they will be able to visit you when they move to Mass.

I think that beginning with the new year I will number my letters so that you will know when there are letters missing. Roy and I number ours and I have a little notebook in which I keep a record of all the letters I write so there should be no difficulty and it might help to keep us straightened out.

I am very pleased with your Christmas shopping for me. It really is wonderful to have you do it for me. I hardly realized that it was Christmas because I wrapped only two gifts, and I really enjoy wrapping presents in the pretty paper and string. Roy might get his gifts by Christmas all right. I still haven't heard from him but I presume there was some delay in the shipping deal. I've seen how the Army and Navy cooperate on the problem of transportation.

Have you seen Cookie lately? Heard a few days ago that Eleanor's husband is in the states so that by now they are no doubt together.

The mail service to me is about the same as you find it there. A few days ago I received mail of Dec. 10, then I receive Nov 25th mail.

That's all for now.

Love.

Pill

27 DECEMBER 1945
ETA JIMA, JAPAN

Dearest Mom and Dad:

Had an enjoyable birthday yesterday. Went over to the engineers for the day. Had a light lunch there.

28 DECEMBER 1945

Dearest Mom and Dad:

I didn't get much written last night did I?

Just got a pile of mail, the first since before Christmas. The cablegram arrived and I was so thrilled to receive it. I will always keep it.

Through the Red Cross we were able to send cable grams but I was afraid it might scare you, or make you think I was arriving home or something so I decided against it. Also received the paper samples from Roy's gifts. It is very pretty. You think of everything.

I will now continue with my discussion of my birthday. After the light lunch we all sat around and listened to the vic and chatted and were really lazy. There were five of us girls there so it was lots of fun. The club had its Christmas dinner that night instead of the night before because the officers had to eat with their enlisted men on Christmas. So I had two big turkey dinners this year. After dinner they presented a movie in the club and we sat around in comfy chairs in the warm room and saw, "Our Vines Grow Tender Grapes".

Just received a letter from the minister in which he announces that for Christmas this year we each receive a years' subscription to the Readers Digest. All I have to do is send him the necessary request.

This place is surely getting dead and empty. We have only 63 patients left, so we are able to send extra nurses off duty every day. As yet I have been unable to benefit from this but I don't mind, in fact I rather enjoy being on duty. My guard keeps me company all the time and I have so very little to do. I'm going to be a secretary when I get home or else a house wife. It's up to Roy, naturally.

Had a card from Jean T. and she wrote a short message on the back telling of Doris receiving her ring and of Walt being in Germany. I can't understand why I never hear from Walt. I don't believe I have heard since I left the states.

The card from Betty Haverly arrived today also and I almost passed out when she said Tuffy Wade was married. I guess I had heard of her being engaged. These things happen.

Bud Welde was over here to see me on my birthday. He missed me and was on his way back to Kure on the ferry and we ran into each other. We chatted for about fifteen minutes then we parted. He sent his best regards to you. His ship was at anchor in Kure base for about four days and he was able to get liberty and find his way over here to Alkatraz.

Nothing else of news now I guess.

Love, Pill

30 DECEMBER 1945

Dearest Mom and Dad:

Just a brief note to go with the enclosed. Hope it goes thru the mail O. K. The picture is self explanatory. I generally wear that outfit, with the pockets full as you can see.

I sent a copy of the picture with a hanky to Net and Irving, and Midge and Dave, (and Roy of course).

Have my radio working in my room, but can't have the light on too. It doesn't bother me because I'm always working in the evening.

No news concerning our next move after the hospital closes January 4. We may return stateside sooner than we expect. I'm sure we'll be back by summer. Due to my being on limited service I will be eligible for discharge when I return, whether or not I stay in the service or not depends on a lot of things.

Excuse my using both sides of the paper. I'm afraid the envelope is going to be too full. I'm feeling fine these days. Think I am going to go to Hiroshima tomorrow if we can get the necessary passes.

Be good and keep your chins up.

Love,

Pauline

Professional Japanese photo of Lt. Denman

LETTERS FROM TINIAN 1945

Dearest Mom and Dad:

And what did you do on New Years' Eve?

I went to a party and had an enjoyable time, but I was awfully lonesome for Roy, especially since I still haven't heard from him.

I didn't have to work New Years eve or New Years night. There are only two nurses on each shift so we don't have to go to work very often. I have to report for duty at four tomorrow but there may not be any patients by then.

Still don't know what we are going to do next.

Went to Hiroshima the other day. I was beginning to wonder if I'd ever see the place. Took the camera along of course. Some day I may have some pictures of it to show you. It is impossible to put into words the destruction caused by that one small yet powerful bomb. We went up onto the roof of the city hall, one of the few buildings still standing and took pictures. The inside of the building was all shattered and burned, but the cement walls and stairways were O. K.

Nothing else to report. Still no snow. Still chilly out, but our stoves keep us fairly warm in our rooms.

I won't laugh at you for dressing warm. I wear long drawers constantly. Don't know what I'd do without them.

Love and kisses,

Pill

P. S. Thanks for the wonderful Christmas shopping you did. No more packages yet—maybe later. Christmas will last a long time this year.

Lt. Denman with friends Hiroshima rooftop

Hiroshima

ETA JIMA
2 JANUARY 1946
LETTER #2

Dearest Mom and Dad,

Just a brief note to let you know I received my Christmas box from you in the mail this P. M.

I enjoyed all the pretty packages and their contents. The pajamas are beautiful and I'll love to wear them this spring and summer. The gift from Maude was a rubber bathing cap. I can use it in the shower as I've been without one for some time.

The crossword puzzle book is adorable. Thanks a million to both of you for the nice presents. You're so nice.

Today I received two letters from the states dated 20 November, and about three days ago I received mail from Seattle dated 21 December. Mail service is crazy.

That's all for now,

Love,

Pauline

The following letter was written on the back of a birthday greeting card.

6 JANUARY 1946

Dearest Mom and Dad,

I know it isn't anyone's birthday but I'm using this to protect the few enclosed snaps. Not much to look at. I'll have some more prints some other time.

Nothing new here. Had a card from Mim Buchaca—she is in nurses' training at Johns' Hopkins in Baltimore, Md.

Heard from the Bantas and Packards.

Love,

8 JANUARY 1946
ETA JIMA, JAPAN
LETTER #3

Dearest Mom and Dad.

We may be on the move again within ten days. Rumor of course. Some say we might even go home, (via the Panama Canal).

I'd like to go from here to China, then India, Egypt, Italy, France, Germany, England and New York via plane with stop overs one or two days each.

Remember that picture I sent of me in a photo studio sitting down looking silly and laughing. The studio has a copy of that picture that they are using as advertisement—to scare the customers away I guess.

They say General Eisenhower is due here Thursday. I'd surely like to see him.

Today I mailed two packages home. No telling when they'll arrive. I might even get there first. They might never arrive. They contain some odds and ends for my hope (less) chest, Jap souvenirs, etc. I also mailed some photos of Miya Jima, the shrine island, yesterday.

Still no word from Roy. I'm pretty worried.

I'm going to the P. O. now so I'll close.

Love,

Pauline

ETA JIMA, JAPAN
9 JANUARY 1946
LETTER #4

Dearest Mom and Dad,

Glad to know the cards and money arrived safely. I was kinda worried but I took the chance.

Still no mail from Roy. I can't understand it.

Four of the nurses left for home today. They had signed up for the duration when they were eligible for discharge, but since the unit is breaking up, they changed their minds and are going home.

We all signed papers last week to be relieved of active duty as soon as possible, or did I tell you before?

I just wrote to Maude and John.

I'm going to have to get a large photo album when I get home to accommodate all the pictures I have. Hope the pictures get through to you O. K.. I am going to buy a set of pictures around here if they have any left tomorrow.

By now you should have the Tinian album. I had one sent to Midge and Dave, and Net and Irving, I think. I can't remember too well, it was so long ago.

Expect to leave here in less than a week—but no official confirmation as yet concerning the matter.

Love,

Pill

10 JANUARY 1946
LETTER #5

Dearest Mom and Dad,

Just a quickie. The list just went up as to who goes but not when. The majority of us are going to Osaka and join the 307th General Hospital. The rest are going to various hospitals in Tokyo. I'm glad I've been assigned to Osaka because the majority of my friends are going there.

If I don't write for a few days, it will be due to packing, etc.

The enclosed are some more pictures from here and there. Guess I'll have to get a huge album to accommodate all these pictures. When I get stateside I'll be busy a month with the pictures alone.

Hope you don't mind getting all this stuff. I dread packing again. It's such a problem because I do have so much junk.

That's all for now.

Love,

Pauline

ETA JIMA JAPAN
11 JANUARY 1946

Dearest Mom and Dad,

Not much to say except that I received a letter from Roy's mother today announcing the fact that Roy and Maggie were married December 20 in Detroit.

Guess that's about all for now. I know he'll never be happy without me. But I can get along without him because I have a lot on the ball and can get almost any man I want if he is worth having.

Love,

Pill

"DEAR JOHN"

This was a "Dear John" letter. I am sure you know what a "Dear John" letter is.

In case you don't, it's the kind of letter a lot of GIs' got from their girls or sometimes even their wives back home when they had found someone new and would no longer be waiting for them to return from war. Pretty cruel but that is the way it is and was and continues to be now that the war is over.

"Mail call" is an important time of day to all of us. Just to know how things are back home and all the nitty gritty. And the mail never arrives in order of its being mailed. Happiness is just getting some mail when far from home. But a "Dear John" letter can throw the recipient into a real, deep funk.

I guess what I got was a "Dear Jane" letter as I am a female

So here I am reading a "Dear Jane" letter,—from his MOM!!!

What I did after reading that isn't fit to print but I did wrap myself around a bottle of Japanese wine. And life goes on.

Charcoal sketch of Lt. Denman by a patient

ETA JIMA
SUNDAY 13 JAN
LETTER # 6

Dear Mom and Dad,

We're leaving for Osaka tomorrow at 8 A. M. My packing is all done except my bedding which I can't pack until the A. M.

I'm enclosing $20.00 again to get rid of it. It's no good over here and I have too much money right now.

I have nothing to do all day and we are restricted to the island. From now on (for a few weeks anyway) my address will be 307th General Hospital, A. P. O. 660, so you might as well start using it.

I wonder what is in store for us in Osaka. You can probably see it on the map next to Kobe, north of here. They say it is a little more civilized there. It's all so primitive where we have been so far. Maybe there will be something interesting to do.

We have to go on duty Tuesday A. M. which is a stinking deal since we will be on the train about eight hours. I think we all will stage a sit down strike. The Jap transportation system is very poor, cold, slow and crowded and we'll be eating rations.

I'll write as soon as we get there.

Love,

Pill

OSAKA, JAPAN
14 JANUARY . MONDAY

Dear Mom and Dad,

Just a note. We arrived safe and sound at the 307th General Hospital. We have nice rooms with steam heat and I am roasting.

Arrived after dark but this looks more like a modern city with paved streets, streetcars, street lights, etc., not like the slums of Kure.

The train ride was warm and comfortable in a special train for just us nurses.

It seems we don't have to go on duty in the A. M. It's a good thing because I'm mighty tired. It's 11:30 P. M.. We arrived here about 9 P. M. having pulled out of Kure, R.R. station at noon.

Good night for now,

Love,

Pill

OSAKA, JAPAN
17 JANUARY 1946 #8

Dearest Mom and Dad,

Today makes six months of overseas service—not that I've done anything to deserve the extra pay of being overseas.

Started work yesterday, on the day shift but there was very little at all to do. We have two half days off a week.

Went to an engineers officers club last evening and had a not too interesting time. The man who took care of my comfort was a nice young good looking Captain—a doctor, with a wife and baby and mustache. He and I spent the evening playing duets on a small organ. He says he can teach me to play in five lessons. I played by ear last night referring to the music occasionally. Frankly I'd rather stay in and read. (I'm reading, "Hungry Hill" by Daphne DeMaurer. It is quite interesting.) He wants me to come over tonight but it's too much bother.

Spent all day Tuesday unpacking and fixing our room up and we are very proud of the result;—in fact everyone else comes in to admire.

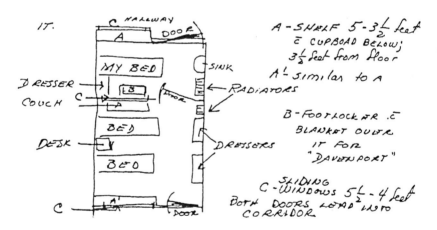

Don't know if you can make it out from the diagram. The walls are freshly painted cream color. I have a pink and white satin spread on my bed. On "A" I have a royal blue shiny material with biege linen gathered skirt. There are floor length drapes (white) with blue tie backs on the window adjoining the two rooms. There are no windows in that opening so I'm not alone. We have white drapes over the other windows and the two hall doorways. The radiator in my room has an oven like business built in the top where I heat water. It is always so warm in here that I sit around in bra and pants.

PAULINE D. WEBB, (LT. PAULINE A. DENMAN, A. N. C. WWII)

I have the double frame with your two pictures on "A" at one end and the snap of you two at 1095 Winton Road at the other end. The room is very livable so we probably won't stay long.

The sixty-five nurses who really belong to the 307th are due to arrive any minute—seven arrived this P. M.; and then we will no doubt be sent elsewhere.

Most of us girls have twelve points. Some eight point nurses went home from the Phillipines having been declared surplus. It's a wonder they don't do the same with us.

I work on a medical ward. All the patients have hepatitis. Most of the patients are not new to me because they were transferred from Eta Jima when we closed. There seems to be an awful lot of cases of hepatitis in the army. I'd like to read up on it and find out why. I went to a medical conference on hepatitis yesterday but arrived too late to get the etiology discussion.

This hospital is large—three five story wings.

Some bombs were dropped close to the building and destroyed the plumbing system. We live in "C", fourth floor and the only john we can use now is in wing "A". I'm still using my helmet for washing purposes. I'd be lost without it.

Life at present is at a low ebb and there is nothing or no one of interest in these parts. I have a blind date tomorrow night and may go to a party Saturday.

Four different organizations are giving parties this Saturday and all have big posters here trying to lure us over—the air corps, infantry, engineers and medics. Don't know which or if I'll go to any yet. There is a boy named Gus from Kure, who is now in Kobe, that I'd give a million to go out with but Kobe is not too near. He wanted a date with me but I was dating his company commander so he didn't dare. That's life, I guess. His company commander (Frankie) is on his way home so I'm keeping my fingers crossed. I doubt if he'll come over.

Rumor: nurses on limited service may go home soon. I'm not too anxious any more. There are an awful lot of extra nurses in Japan.

This letter is getting awfully long and I have some washing and ironing to do.

Did I tell you I've been wearing my two piece green brief pajamas around the room here?

Love,

Pauline

21 JANUARY 1946
OSAKA, JAPAN
LETTER #9

Dearest Mom and Dad,

Here I am on detached service again—98th Field Hospital here in Osaka. We are still quartered at the 307th General Hospital. We are transported over here, only a couple of blocks, via truck. Twenty of us were sent here, having been notified yesterday. I only hope they don't decide to have us move over here. I'm so well satisfied with our living quarters.

Received mail yesterday for the first time since our arrival in Osaka. Rev. Rothermal is an old nurse who has been in Laborador and many other places in missionary work. When we were in training she used to bore us for hours with her tales of her travels. I'll never bore people by telling of my travels, except you perhaps. The blonde baby's picture is a boy born on my birthday last year at Ft. Monmouth. Am anxious to see it because he was my pride and joy and so very handsome. Received the Christmas card today that you mailed November 23. Heard from the Fergusons. Doug is due in the states in a few weeks and I think he plans to return to R. P. I.. Had letters from Alta, Charles and Jimmy. Heard from Rev. Brandt and received a religious magazine from the Ladies Aid.

We were re-vaccinated again yesterday. There are quite a few cases of small pox in Kobe and I'm mighty glad of the vaccination.

Was quite relieved today to receive a letter from Roy written on the day he arrived in the states. I couldn't understand his failure to write re the matter; it was so unlike him. The letter was post marked December 3. I quote parts of it: "I am sorry to have to tell you so coldly and believe that you could talk me out of it if you were here . . . . my change of heart was intensified by learning that between Maggie and my mother the wedding details had been completely arranged . . . .Realize that you are better off to be rid of one who doesn't know his own mind. Admittedly I am going into marriage "without love", but then I am not too sure what love is anyway . . ."

So ends another chapter in the life and loves of "Pill".

Met an awfully nice 2nd Lt. at an officer's club the other night. My problem is how to "shake" the doc (the one with wife, baby and mustache) and go out with the young Lt. (Jones). Life has its little problems. Last night Lt. Jones was sick in bed, so Doc and I went to visit him. I spent 45 minutes steady rubbing his back.

There is also a Lt. Gus Wavpotich (?) in Kobe who is a nice guy.

I'll get along, I guess. I wonder if Roy will. Doug isn't happy without me. Neither is Hudson. Boy am I conceited. I'll never forget the happiness we knew on Tinian. I don't think I was ever happier with anyone. I'll get over it. The initial shock will wear off soon.

PAULINE D. WEBB, (LT. PAULINE A. DENMAN, A. N. C. WWII)

I'm on a surgical ward now—eight patients, two nurses on duty. I'm on 7-3 for the next two weeks

There isn't much more to write now. Excuse paper, I'm on the ward and this is the best I can do.

Love,

Pill

Lt. Frederick S. Jones (nickname d "Boxcar")

Lt. August Anthony Wavpotich "Gus"

OSAKA, JAPAN
25 JANUARY 1946
LETTER #10

Dearest Mom and Dad,

Guess I have been neglecting my letter writing of late. Nothing new to report. Am still working at the 98th Field Hospital and living at the 307th. The weather has been rainy and mild this week.

I have a cold so I've been staying in evenings and forcing fluids. It's the first cold I've had which is amazing because everyone had colds back on Eta Jima.

This is my day off for the week and I'm going to go through the historic castle with Paul (Dr. Dillihunt) this afternoon.

I went to Kobe the other evening and had a very enjoyable time with my old flame Gus from Kure, who is now stationed in Kobe. The building that their club is in is the first real stateside building I've been in, with revolving doors (to the left—not right—in Japan), took an elevator to the 8th floor, walked down a marble hallway. Looked just like New York. The dining hall was georgeous—red plaid table cloth and napkins.

Two of our girls are leaving today to go stateside on emergency leaves, trouble at home I guess, being the cause.

Did I tell you about the jobs some of the girls are doing instead of nursing—working in the P.X., post office, kitchen, registrar's office and personnel office. We nurses are very versatile.

Managed to get some powdered milk and powdered malted milk from one of the girls in the kitchen so I have hot malted milk anytime I wish and it's very good. I boil the water on my radiator. Last night we all had fried eggs and beef sandwiches in one of the kids rooms. It pays to have nurses work in the kitchen. The meals at the 98th field hospital have been very good. Steak one day, roast turkey with dressing the next day.

Heard from Midge yesterday with Doris picture enclosed. Received your letters with the embroidery cotton enclosed. Mucho gracia. Am glad to know that the colored "portrait" arrived safely. Did you really recognize me?

Am anxious to see all the new paper and drapes, etc. I won't know the place when I get there.

I haven't heard from Cookie in quite some time. I hope she is feeling O.K. Elsie wrote that Dr. Donhauser is going to get married again.

That's all for now I guess.

Love,

Pill

The castle, an army garrison was built in 1928 to commemerate
Hirohito's enthronement. It sits on the foundation of a fort built in
1583. Kilroy was here.

KILROY WAS HERE

As it didn't appear in any of the letters, the mention of , "Kilroy was Here" should not be omitted. I remember being surprised to see it when I was in Osaka Castle although I shouldn't have been surprised as the occupation troops had started arriving in Japan long before I got there.

This simple graffiti captured the imagination of GI's everywhere they went. He was the one who always got there first and who was always there when they left. Legends abound about its origin.

The legend of how it started is with James J. Kilroy, a shipyard inspector during WWII. He chalked the words on bulkheads to show that he had been there and inspected the riveting in the newly constructed ship.

Kilroy became the US Super-GI who always got there first, wherever GI's went. It became a challenge to place the logo in the most unlikely places, i. e. atop Mt Everest, the Statue of Liberty, the underside of the Arch de Triumphe etc.

An outhouse was built for the exclusive use of Truman, Stalin and Churchill who were there for the Potsdam conference. The first person to use it was Stalin. He emerged and asked his aide (in Russian), "Who is Kilroy?"

And so the stories go.

Who's That Again? *Yotaro Kazama, a simple Japanese making the traditional pilgrimage up 12,467-foot Mount Fuji, pauses in the hard climb to puzzle over the ubiquitous memento of a previous visitor.*

OSAKA, JAPAN 27 JANUARY 1946
LETTER # 11 (-1)

Dearest Mom and Dad,

Here I am on duty, my work now completed for a few minutes. It's pouring outside, and I have a heavy date with Gus at 1 P. M. Had a heavy date last night 210 pounds, 6 feet 1 ½ inches, handsome and with a Boston accent, and a smooth dancer, a football player from the University of Maine.

Rumor: fifteen point nurses leaving in a few days for the states; twelve pointers leaving by 1 March, (I have 12 points).I would like to take advantage of the G. I. Bill but don't know what to study or what school I would want to attend.

Went through the famous Osaka Castle. Six flights of stairs. Not very impressive inside. It had been used as a museum before the war. Our trip to Kyoto is pending. May go this week on my day off. I'll be going with the doctor I guess and another couple.

It was just like spring out the last two days. Nice and warm. My cold is gone already. This climate seems to be good for my usually chronic colds.

No one of our outfit at all is left on Eta Jima, so it looks like the mail situation will be bad. I'm so anxious to get my packages. I ordered a pink skirt and dark shirts last August from a store in N. J.. The order was mailed from there on 28 September. I wish they'd come and my shoes too. I really need them. You have to have new clothes once in a while.

The plumbing situation got so bad in our quarters that we had to resort to the outside latrine like on Tinian. We really appreciated it.

Went to the "New Osaka Hotel" for the dance last night. Just like going to the Astor Roof in New York City. Nothing like a few months overseas to make you really appreciate stuff.

Gotta go now, Love, Pill

In some of my prior letters I mentioned Capt. Paul H. Dillahunt, Gus and Lt. Jones. I would like to elucidate a bit about them. They were all nice gentlemen. They wrote on my "short snorter".

LETTERS FROM TINIAN 1945

SHORT SNORTERS

A *"short snorter"* is a little less than a full drink at a bar. During World War II a short snorter was a chain of paper currency taped together end to end. It usually inferred that the owner had crossed the Equator but not necessarily.

I had not crossed the Equator but had crossed the International Date Line. My short snorter is about five or six feet long. And starts with a U. S. one dollar bank note with Hawaii stamped across the back. The rest of the bank notes are from various countries I had visited or notes that had been given to me by others.

If you failed to have your short snorter with you, you were stuck with the tab for a round of all those present. We would have friends and colleagues sign our notes.

One of the signatures I have is " Capt. Paul H. Dillahunt" who was mentioned earlier, in Osaka as, " a nice, young, good looking Captain – a doctor, with a wife and baby and mustache".

Shortly after moving to Jacksonville I saw in the paper an item about a local doctor. Paul H. Dillahunt. That not being a common name I wrote to him to see if he was the gentleman I had known in Japan.

In reply I received the following:

4/29/89

Dear Ms Webb,

I was born in 1948 so WWII was a bit before my time.

My father served in the Army Medical Corps in WWII and probably is the person to whom you are referring.

He can be reached at (I am deleting the phone number) in Columbus, Ohio. Maybe you could call him. He would probably enjoy talking to you.

PHD II

I find that writing letters is easy, but phone calls floor me so I never called him.
Seven years later I again wrote to the local Dr. Dillahunt as follows

24 June 1996

Dear Dr. Dillahunt,

I am enclosing a copy of the kind letter you wrote in 1989 to help you recall the incident. I was too chicken to call your dad.

PAULINE D. WEBB, (LT. PAULINE A. DENMAN, A. N. C. WWII)

Currently I am preparing a book that I hope to publish and would like to talk to or write to your dad if he is still living.

I am also enclosing a copy of the short snorter on which he signed his name.

Thanking you for your kindness, I am,

Sincerely yours,

A few days later I received this reply:

Dear Ms Webb,

That appears to be his signature. I recognize his writing. He is still living and again I encourage you to contact him. He is really a nice guy!

PHD II

Again I was chicken and didn't call. I regret that I didn't follow thru.

Another name on my short snorter was Gus. He wrote, "Stateside to the core and blonde"
Lt. Gus Wavpotich. After the war we planned to meet and play some tennis. He was going to change his name to John August Brooks and return to Pratt Institute in Brooklyn and finish his art studies. He returned stateside to California and we lost touch.

My short snorter was signed on many of the bills by Roy with various messages. There are many other signatures I can barely read and not remember at all. But the one by Fred S. Jones (Boxcar) brings back a few memories. He went back to the Univ. Of Maine in Orono to get his engineering degree and I flew up there for several week end parties and he visited me in Ithaca but our relationship finally faded as those things do after a while. I met Boxcar when he was sick in Osaka and Dr Dillahunt and I made a "house call" and I gave him a back rub.

Part of the short snorter

30 JANUARY 1946
OSAKA, JAPAN
LETTER # 11

Dearest Mom and Dad,

No news around here, just the usual rumors. Latest—ten point nurses going stateside very, very soon. I have twelve points.

I'm on duty now and my mind is a complete blank as to what to write.

I start a two week shift of 3-11 starting Saturday night, of all nights. I will be on a different ward much to my displeasure.

We have a patient on this ward from Waits River, Vermont with six toes on each foot. What a dope he is. His accent is very familiar however. He used to have twelve fingers but they got in the way so he cut them off.

Mail service is again very poor and I'm getting awfully anxious about my packages. I need the clothes and would like to have my pumps so I could sharp up evenings for my new conquest.

I still haven't been able to finish my book, "Hungry Hill". I was C. Q. (Charge of quarters) night before last and wore myself out. Haven't played bridge in a while so I think I'll try to cook up a game tonight. Maybe a game of Cribbage for a change. Haven't played since I left Tinian. We used to play it by the hour. I'm no doubt rusty by now.

This surely is dull reading. Rainy weather for the last four days. No curls. No snow. No scenery. No news. Forgive me if my letter numbering is a little off at times.

Love, Pill

OSAKA, JAPAN

2 FEBRUARY 1946

LETTER # 12

Dearest Mom and Dad,

Here I am on duty again with nothing to do and nothing to write at all. I'm working 3-11 and have four wards, all isolation – twenty patients in all with syphilis or diphtheria, nothing else. Rather a dull place at present.

Today's rumor – leaving within two weeks for the states. Seeing is believing and I haven't seen it in print yet.

I have an important dinner date tomorrow and my dress isn't back from the cleaners. It's been there two weeks now and it should have been back before now. Looks like I am going to have to keep wearing my suit until I get stateside. Maybe it won't be long now. Haven't worn a dress since Tinian days. Weather is usually too cold.

Hope you will forgive me for forgetting to remember to number these letters when I get back to my room.

Haven't had any mail at all for a week I guess. I don't go to the post office very often anyway.

Met an old fraternity brother of Dave's from Union College. Maybe you remember his name – Doug Blue. He used to date Nancy Wagner. He's a Captain in the engineers in Osaka. He's changed a lot – in six years I guess he should. We had a nice long chat about all our friends, etc. Small world.

Can't think of anything else to write about.

Since there is no Kresges here, I'll have to wish you a Happy Valentine's Day.

Love, Pill

OSAKA, JAPAN
8 FEBRUARY 1946
(LETTER # 13)

Dearest Mom and Dad,

Life is at a very slow ebb around these parts. All I do is sleep and work 3-11 and I don't work. There is nothing to do except a few shots, temps and back rubs

Things aren't nice like they were on Eta Jima. It is just a dirty, bombed out city.

Last night it snowed a couple of hours and was quite nice but it melted as fast as it landed.

Saw a Japanese show here in the hospital the other evening. It was comparable to what would have passed for a good show in the states in 1930 – the songs, costumes and music were all outdated. Very corny indeed.

Tonight I went to a movie they showed here in the auditorium, a Rita Hayworth musical.

The rumor is still going around that us twelve pointers will be on stateside orders very soon, in fact momentarily.

Had three letters this week – two from you folks and one from Mae Souder. Haven't heard from Cookie in quite some time. Hope all is well with her and her hubby.

Guess I better cut this short as I am in a blue mood. And that is very rare these days because I am generally in very high spirits.

Be good and don't work too hard and I'll be home soon.

Love,

"Pill".

ON DUTY
9 FEBRUARY 1946

Dearest Mom and Dad,

Just a note. At supper tonight they said all twelve pointers were relieved of duty as of noon tomorrow and that we will leave here about Tuesday.

Don't know how long it will be before we get on stateside transportation. It's all so sudden that it scares me. Once I get stateside I'll have a lot of decisions to make. I haven't even been in service eighteen months. Maybe I'll stay in a while, I don't know. I'll have a lot of time to think when I get out of here.

I'll be spending all day tomorrow with Gus in Kobe. I might even run into him again stateside since he is a New Yorker too.

Guess my packages will never come now. An awful lot of things must be either at the bottom of the ocean or else in the wrong hands.

That's all for now.

Love, "Pill"

14 FEBRUARY 1946
BE MY VALENTINE
14

Dearest Mom and Dad,

With mail service being what it is today, I might arrive before this letter. I'll wire you as soon as I hit the states. We will probably go to Seattle.

We're at the 4th Replacement Depot in Yokohama. We left Osaka Tuesday and arrived in Nagoya late that evening. Upon arrival there at the 11th Replacement Depot our orders were changed and they sent us up here last night via Pullman, arriving at 5:15 A. M.—then an hour and a half truck ride in the cold, cold air to the depot here. I think we will leave within the week, sometime after Saturday.

Was tempted to surprise you and not let you know I was coming home, but I am afraid you might worry if you don't hear.

My plans for the future are very unsettled. I would like to go to school but don't know where, or what to study.

I'm not positive of my eligibility for discharge. We're reporting to Fort Dix and then go on leave I presume. Don't know much concerning the matter as you can see.

Don't worry if you don't hear from me. I should be home by the end of March, but you can't be sure of anything in the army and it's transportation.

Am anxious to see the new wallpaper and drapes.

According to the newspaper, only one letter in six goes via air mail to the states. Mail service is highly inadequate either way. Guess I'll never get my packages now.

Be good. Keep the home fires burning and the welcome mat out

Love, Pill

Well that is the end of the letters, but not the end of the story. I carefully folded the letters, put them back in the envelopes, tied them back up with the ribbons and put them safely away, for my heirs, an historian or whomever might be interested.

HOMEWARD BOUND

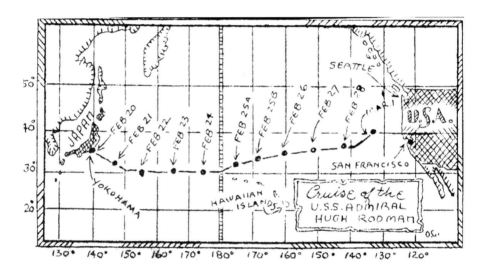

LIFTED ANCHOR 20 FEB 0800
1945

TROOPSHIPS DUE TODAY

At Seattle
USS Admiral Redman from
Yokohama, 4,707 Army, including
eight generals

PAULINE A DENMAN

To you who answered the call of your country and served in its Armed Forces to bring about the total defeat of the enemy, I extend the heartfelt thanks of a grateful Nation. As one of the Nation's finest, you undertook the most severe task one can be called upon to perform. Because you demonstrated the fortitude, resourcefulness and calm judgment necessary to carry out that task, we now look to you for leadership and example in further exalting our country in peace.

Harry Truman

PART II

EPILOGUE

After returning stateside, we shipped directly to Ft. Dix, New Jersey, a separation center. Upon arrival I received my promotion to First Lt., surprising to some extent because some of the others in my group did not receive a promotion. They had been to the PX to get their silver bars in anticipation of the raise in rank, believing it would be automatic on return from overseas.

From there I returned to my parents' home in Delmar, N Y, a suburb of Albany, the Capitol, to spend my final leave and return to civilian hospital nursing. I debated the pros and cons of going back to school under the G. I. Bill. I elected not to return to school to get my B. S. in nursing or other studies. Perhaps later I would consider it after further reflection

Shortly after returning to stateside nursing, I was on a private case at Albany Hospital when I was summoned to the office of the Nursing Supervisor. (A scary thought!). Upon arriving at her office I was graciously invited to come in and asked to sit down. After a short discussion about me and about my position. (I was an employee of a nursing agency , not of the hospital), she asked if I was free and willing to fly to Minneapolis, Minn to work at the Polio Emergency Hospital at Ft. Snelling, working for the Red Cross.

I hesitated and delayed my answer for a few days. There were loose ends to address. One being the case I was on and the other being a relationship I was in with Howie.

When I was home on my final leave my sister called me from Boston where she was working at the Harvard Biological Lab as a secretary and her husband was a graduate student at the Harvard Graduate College of Education. She invited me to come for a visit and hitch a ride with Howie. Howie was a friend of hers and a member of her wedding party to Dave. I knew him and didn't like him. I don't know why, did he tease me, did he ignore me? For whatever reason I did not like him and was reluctant to call him up, so my mom did. He was driving a friend to Boston and would be happy to have another passenger. So it came to pass, with me riding in the back seat and being dropped off at my sister's house in Lexington, Mass.

On the return trip I sat in the front seat and it wasn't too bad. The radio was playing, "South of the Border" and he was singing along, etc.. We got along just fine and after that, started dating. We joined a bowling league, played poker with the members of the bowling league, etc. He was a widower with a two year old son. I went to Howie Jrs second birthday party and gave him a framed embroidery piece I had created (I don't remember the verse) to hang on his wall.

I told him about my plans to go to Minnesota and he didn't try to deter me. So I formulated plans to go. Soon I was on my first airplane flight. I had been in the army, overseas, and in many types of transportation, had been in a B-29 but had never flown , so this was a thrilling adventure. I got dumped in Chicago from over booking (although I was on an emergency trip for the Red Cross). They soon found me a connecting flight. And without too much delay I was at work with all these children who had had polio and were there for treatment. I was assigned night duty so I was not present when the children got their treatment. Primarily they were using the Kenny method of hot packs to relieve the spasaming muscles. Sister Kenny was an Australian nurse who had devised a method of treating polio patients. She was neither a nurse nor a nun but earned the title "sister" while working with the Austrailian Medical Corps during World War One. Her methods were not readily accepted by the medical community but they were very successful.

While I was there, Sister Kenny came for a visit with two Hollywood film stars Barbara Hale and her husband Bill Williams. I don't know why except perhaps in preparation for a film to be made. A film was subsequently made starring Rosalind Russell.

I stayed several months in Minneapolis and made many friends and visited the twin cities. Howie and I were corresponding during that time. But soon he met a new girl, Agnes, whom he finally married. Upon my return to Albany, he met me at the rail road station in Albany and drove me home but our "romance" was all over. I rejoined the bowling league and returned to work. I finally met Agnes, and I was not impressed – I thought Howie liked well dressed sophisticated women but Agnes wore ankle socks with high heels!! How strange a way to make a judgment.

A few years later I moved with my parents to Ithaca, NY where I met and married my first husband, Leonard. After his death from Hodgkins Disease I married Cecil Webb the father of our two children. We made our home in Ithaca for nearly twenty years. Two years after we moved to Florida he died of a heart attack. So I was left with two children ages 11 and 14 and soon had to return to nursing

One evening as I was going out the door on my way to work, the phone rang It was Howie and I said, "Howie who?" It had been a long , long time and I didn't immediately remember who Howie was. He was in Miami at a PTA convention or meeting. He and Agnes had about six children so I am sure he was quite active in the PTA. I wasn't interested in seeing him so I cut the conversation short and left for work. Back in Delmar if he had asked, I would have married him instead of going to Minneapolis. I was quite fond of him and ready to settle down.

DELMAR, NEW YORK

Delmar, New York was a wonderful town, it was in fact one of three little towns called the Tri-Village area, population total 3000. I lived there from about 1928 until a few years after the war when it was still a wonderful little town. Perhaps that is what the town of one's youth always is, the best. The town had one stop light, and one cop, Dave Main. It had a volunteer fire department, the first one to arrive drove the truck. I remember an old iron (steel?) ring about four feet in diameter hanging near the main thoroughfare that was used to call the fire department by striking it with a hammer or mallet.

The stop light was at the "Four Corners" so called, the main intersection even though there were five corners. I lived a block away from the stoplight where we had dirt sidewalks, and when the town put in cement walks I was so thrilled to have a place to ride my scooter bike. The only decent place to roller skate was in front of the bank which had a wide paved area. I really prized my scooter bike, a two wheeler. As kids do, I used to leave it out by the birch trees at the end of the driveway (instead of bringing it up to the front porch or putting it in the garage). One day I went out to get it and it was gone, having been replaced by a kids wagon. The mystery was soon solved when a man came looking for his son who had run away from home with his little wagon. His home was Slinglerlands another village several miles away. We all got in his car and soon found the lad and my bike. All was well.

Once my sister and I were going to run away (why?). We were going upstairs to the den, crawl out the window and out onto the back porch roof, then down the trellis. We had our sweaters on the newel post , ready to take on our journey, but my eagle eyed mother spotted the sweaters and questioned the reason for them being there. And that was the end of it. Perhaps the coming of darkness made home look pretty good after all.

My first big romance was in Delmar in the second grade. When I entered the room the first day of second grade I chose a seat next to a cute little boy wearing blue shorts. His name was Jackie Brookins. I don't remember what went on that year, but when I was in third grade I had a seat at the back of one of the rows near the door. Every time he returned to the room from errands or whatever he would kiss me on the back of the neck. When at parties I remember a lot of kisses in a closet. But he moved away to the city. Years later there was a human interest story in the Albany Times Union about a boy whose dog was run over by a car and his picture was in the paper. It was Jackie. Shortly after seeing it in the paper a friend and I rode our bikes into Albany and hunted him down and visited him. A few weeks later at Easter his father drove him to Delmar to deliver to me an Easter basket. That is the last contact I had with him. When next I heard about him was again from the paper , he had been involved in a minor crime and went into the army instead of jail. End of report.

Dad always made us play outdoors, no matter how deep the snow, or how cold or hot. He said he didn't want to raise hot house flowers. We enjoyed many activities I am sure no longer occupy children. We played marbles, hop scotch, jump rope, cowboys and Indians, hours in the woods in an old sandy area, climbing and bending Birches. We played a lot of cowboys and Indians. Dad made a covered wagon out of our cart, mom providing the canvas (an old sheet). We played pirates and made a Jolly Roger flag to make it real, we created a Fourth of July Parade for our street. We created fun and played outdoors.

We didn't have much money, it was back in the 30's. One source of money was picking bugs off the grape vines. A penny for every 25 bugs. I remember taking my little can of crank case oil and dropping the bugs in and counting carefully. What allowance I remember getting went into my savings on bank day at school. The class that had the highest percentage of depositors each week would get the flag. I remember having a twenty-five cent coin from Canada that I cherished so I deposited it on bank day thinking it was safe there and I would get it back someday.

I remember bringing home frogs and toads and snakes but the most fun was the polly wogs. We would collect the polly wogs from the pond on the way home from school and keep them until they dropped their tails and grew legs. Then we would have races with them.

In high school there was an organization called, "The Deputies" for students who didn't make the teams and could earn their letters by earning points. The points were awarded for x number of hours or miles in various athletic endeavors , i. e. biking, hiking, playing tennis, etc. I was a member for four years and when I was a Senior I was Captain of the Deputies. It was fun growing up in Delmar. Mothers didn't drive cars, they were always home. Our time wasn't organized for us. We went outside and created fun.

One thing you can't do is "go home again". A drive through Delmar a few years ago was not like it was in the 20s and 30s. The house was smaller and the trees taller and the traffic too heavy. There was so much growth that the tri—villages were part of the city of Albany with no open fields separating them. You just can't go home, except in your mind.

Mostly I remember Delmar looking like the streets in the movie' "To Kill a Mocking Bird". Happy childhoods always leave a memorable picture of how things looked, how things were and the freedom of a brief time in ones life.

ON MY MIND
RANDOM THOUGHTS

Reading these letters for the first time after having written them over fifty years ago was almost like reading a stranger's diary. But they transported me back to that time, that small window of time.

It brings it back so clearly—those days in the middle of a war, in the middle of the Pacific in a war zone, falling in love and going "steady" (where the ratio was forty men per woman). What a dope, but I was in love, in love with Roy.

Except for a brief encounter with Roy in Syracuse, N. Y. shortly after the war, our paths never crossed again. I did keep his letters until I married, keeping a few of the envelopes for my stamp collection. Today I wish I had those letters to read again.

The love and remembrance of Maj. Spencer remain in a corner of my heart. I still have the pen and pencil set he gave me, but mostly I have the memories.

In preparing these letters for publication the only person mentioned in these letters that I tried to contact was Roy O. Spencer. My daughter used her computer to search out any person by that name. She found seven. I wrote to each and every one, receiving answers from them all and none was the one I sought or did they know of him.

Perhaps some day after this is published, I will answer a knock on my front door and find him standing there with that special, lop sided grin on his face, that special charm that stole my heart. It would be nice to know what he did with his life, what paths he took, his joys and sorrows. If he were interested I would tell him about mine.

But finding him on my door step is so remote, a mere fantasy. Those things only happen in the movies.

Knock, knock.

If you are a died-in-the-wool romantic, believe in happy endings, the lovers ride off into the sunset and live happily ever after, don't read any more. Just end it back there where there is a knock on the door.

But if you do choose to read further, here is the rest of the story, i. e. what happened after I finished the manuscript, or thought I had finished the manuscript.

PAULINE D. WEBB, (LT. PAULINE A. DENMAN, A. N. C. WWII)

As I mentioned before, I had been searching for Roy Oscar ever since reading those old letters and putting together the manuscript around those events at the end of the war.

I had not seen him or heard from him, nor even given much thought of him for over fifty years, not since that brief encounter in Syracuse, N. Y. a few years after the war. It wasn't exactly a chance encounter, it was a rendezvous we had planned. I have no memory of what brought about that meeting or how he knew I had moved to Ithaca, N.Y., or how I knew to meet him in Syracuse. It is a total blank.

I had just learned to drive and had bought my first car. I worked and saved for a long time to get enough money to buy a car. I remember standing in the rain at bus stops, waiting at the bus stop for the bus that never came because it was way below zero. I still lived in Delmar, New York and worked at Albany Hospital about five miles away. One morning the highways were all covered with ice and I stayed on the bus beyond my usual bus stop to have a level route to walk to the hospital. Upon arrival, my patient refused to let me do a thing for her until I called my mother to tell her I had arrived safely.

Another patient was secretary to the governor and we had an excellent relationship even after she returned home. Many memorable moments while saving up for that car. I finally had enough cash and bought a 1946 maroon Chevy convertible for $2100.00.

That is the car I drove to Syracuse that day. Having had very little driving experience especially in new cities it was quite an undertaking. I took my eyes off the road briefly to check the map (dumb!!) and looked up to see I had almost rear ended a farm wagon loaded with hay. I never tried that again. Since it was about a sixty mile drive, I had made a room reservation at a hotel and I remember finding the hotel but having to ride around in circles to get to the hotel because of one way streets, etc. Mostly inexperience in driving and a new city to explore made it a bit frustrating.

Of our time together I remember very little. Was he in uniform or business suit? What did we talk about? How did I feel about him, seeing him again? He had another gentleman with him as they were on their way to some meetings elsewhere, so perhaps our personal discussions were limited. We had dinner together and that is all I can remember. He had to leave early the next morning and I returned to Ithaca the next day.

The thing I remember most clearly was pulling into the yard where my dad was standing sharpening his scythe and he was so happy I had made it home safely that he cut his hand on the scythe. He was usually much more careful. He was never demonstrative by giving kisses or hugs, but I knew he cared. and this reinforced it.

The only memory of Roy after that meeting was burning all of his letters,(but oh how I wish I had saved them.) when I was getting ready to get married. For the next fifty years I was much too busy living my life to think of what might have been. I still have his dog tag, the envelopes from some of his letters in my stamp collection, his Cribbage board and the Parker 51 pencil and pen set with his name engraved on it, that he gave me when I shipped out from Tinian, with instructions to practice writing, "Mrs Roy Oscar Spencer . . . I also have the silver I.D. bracelet from the China, Burma, India Theater on the front of which he had scratched, 'PILL" and "ROY" and on the back, "TINIAN' , "7 AUG 45". Also in my jewelry box I have his gold leaf Major insignia pin along with my gold and silver Lt bar pins. No engagement ring, no wedding ring.

THE SEARCH

PAULINE D. WEBB, (LT. PAULINE A. DENMAN, A. N. C. WWII)

After reading all of these letters from the attic, I just wanted to see him one more time. Just to talk to him, just to touch him and see his smile. In the past year I watched a movie called "Forever Young" starring Mel Gibson and Jamie Lee Curtis. It was about two young people in love who became separated and each thought the other had died. Fifty three years later he learned she had not died and searched to find her. He eventually did find out where she was and flew out to her home and they embraced and walked off together arm in arm. As I said, that is the way it is in the movies, but I thought there is always a possibility such things do happen in the real world.

So I became more and more anxious to find him. I did a lot of research in the library. I found a book on "Missing Persons USA", with an Appendix E for "Military Location Addresses" for the various branches of the service. I wrote to both the Army and the Air Force. During the war it was The Army Air Force, but later was changed into two separate branches. I also wrote to the commander of the Pacific War Veterans of America.

It was through the Department of Veterans Affairs, and Mr. William Booth, Veterans Service Officer in St. Petersburg , Florida that I finally got my answer. In a letter dated 26 July 2000 he wrote: "A review of U. S. Department of Veterans Affairs (VA) records reflects that Mr. Spencer passed away on May 26, 1998. That was so cold and impersonal that it just stunned me. I was really heartbroken. I had lost him again. I was just a few years too late

If you keep on living, your story keeps adding up no matter what, so several years later when a letter came from the Veterans Service Office, I was pretty curious. I ripped it open, dropping all my other mail on the floor in my anxiety. I just couldn't believe the contents of the letter. They had made a mistake. SNAFU.!! It was not Roy O.Spencer who had died. It was Mrs. Roy O. Spencer who had passed away That was a really BIG mistake, hard to believe anyone dealing with service records could make such an error.

It took a while for the reality to sink in, and when it did, I started writing letters again. If I were computer savvy I would have done it faster that way , but I can still type and I did. If she had died, he might still be alive. The.only information I was finally able to glean was that he was in the Detroit area in a senior facility. That was something positive. And if it was the right Roy Spencer, perhaps I was on the right track, especially with the middle name of Oscar. That narrowed it down to some extent. But there are hundreds of senior villages in Detroit and the surrounding area.

It took some doing to find out more, especially the actual whereabouts of Roy. Since the advent of Sept 11, 2001 less information is readily available. When it seemed like it was taking forever, having written letter after letter to various sources, using various avenues on the internet, I received the information that he was living in Detroit Senior Village in a cottage with his dog, Major.

Following up on that information., I wrote more letters and finally gleaned as my best source the activities supervisor, (Janice Winter) at Detroit Senior Village, who was quite forthcoming. In answer to one of my letters she wrote:

Dear Ms Webb,

It was nice to hear from you and know one of our almost daily friendly visitors has someone who might bring him cheer, though he seems pretty content. His children and grandchildren visit him often at his cottage and sometimes come here for activities with him.

During one of our many conversations , he mentioned he is still seeking someone with whom to play cribbage and has as yet found no one. He stated that his interest in Cribbage dated back to being on Tinian Island in WWII and playing the game with a certain little blonde nurse. He even gave her his Cribbage board. He has no idea if she is still alive or what her name might be after all these years.

Said she wouldn't be interested in an "old codger" like him even if he found her. I will say he doesn't act like an "old codger". He is spry, very intelligent, and interesting to sit and chat with when others in the social hall are busy with their own interests.

I have talked with his sons on several occasions when they have visited here. They say he rarely mentions the war or his experiences. It was a long time ago and most veterans don't often talk about it unless they are requested to elucidate about their experiences.

I did glean from the sons his experiences and life after the war. He married and had four children, two boys and two girls. When the war ended he decided to make the Air Force his career.

He was stationed at the Pentagon in Washington , D. C. for three years. He was then accepted to the graduate engineering program at the University of Illinois where he completed his Masters Degree in Electrical Engineering.

The army then sent him to Wright Patterson Air Force Base near Dayton, Ohio to teach at the Air Institute. He stayed there for three years. He returned to the University of Illinois to complete his Ph.D in Electrical Engineering and, upon completing his degree, he again taught at the Air Institute at Wright Patterson.

Roy was considered for a teaching position at the new Air Force Academy in Colorado, but his superiors determined he was needed in the field. After about a year in the field Roy decided he would probably not receive a promotion to Colonel, as he had not attended West Point.

He left the Army Air Force in 1958. He stayed in Dayton and went to work for the National Cash Register Company. While working there, he helped design their first computer.

Still wanting to return to teaching, he sent resumes to several schools. He decided to accept an offer from his alma mater, Wayne State University in his hometown of Detroit, Michigan. He taught primarily graduate level courses in Electrical and Computer Engineering.

I hope I have related the information correctly. The sons seemed quite knowledgeable about his career. He certainly is well educated and had a happy career and today seems pretty content with his life. As I said, he doesn't talk much about his past, but ask about his children and grandchildren and you will glean all you want to know.

I will respect your request that he not be told of your inquiry. Thank you again for your interest in one of our group of friends. I look forward to your visit and meeting you.

Sincerely,

Janice Winter, Recreation Dept.

Receiving that letter certainly was confirmation that I had found the right Roy Spencer. I was so excited that I called up Deb and told her about it. Deb was equally excited about the information in the letter and suggested that I start writing to him and setting up some dialogue. I decided to think about it for a while. Deb does get pretty excited about my interests and activities.

I remember the time when I lived in south Florida and was visiting Deb in Jacksonville. I visited often and usually came when she was performing in a ballet. We were looking for something interesting to do when she had time off and decided to go to some "Open Houses". She was trying to get me interested in moving to Jacksonville as she had just purchased a home here. I always liked looking at houses but had no intention of relocating. I was still working as a nurse and owned my own home in Coconut Creek, Florida.

However we did visit an interesting house in a nice neighborhood, and Deb was so intrigued and especially interested in the library with floor to ceiling book shelves, that she tried to persuade me to buy it and move up to be near her, using bribery, i.e. "If you buy it, I'll rip up all the old carpet and refinish the hardwood floors," etc.. So I bought the house on the spur of the moment, either that day or the next. And she never redid my floors, they were in perfect condition. She lucked out, but then she got stuck with me.

At Sunday breakfast here with Deb and Sam, I decided to run an idea by them. "What do you think about the idea of me hopping a plane and flying to Detroit for a surprise visit?"

"Mom, you aren't serious. I can hardly get you to leave the house to go to the ballet."

Sam spoke up between bites of grits and runny eggs, "Deb, I think she means it and really would go."

Deb immediately spoke up, "Mom, I'll drive you to the airport. I'll take care of your house and the cats. Go for it!"

"Deb, you are my "social secretary" , you can make the reservations for June and I will write to Miss Winter.

Shortly thereafter, I wrote to Janice Winter asking her if she thought it would be prudent for me to fly up there and visit Roy perhaps in June. I would like to do it without letting him know. Could he handle the shock and surprise.

In due time I received this reply:

Dear Ms. Webb

I have your letter and your suggestion to visit in June. I am sure Mr. Spencer will be delighted to see you and he is capable of withstanding the shock and excitement.

When you have your travel plans formulated let us know and we will send a car to pick you up at the airport. I will also find a way to make sure Mr. Spencer is here on that date.

We don't have too much excitement on a daily basis and this will bring us all a high that should last for quite a while.

Now don't get cold feet about coming as you hinted at in your letter. Formulate your plans and keep me posted. I expect to hear from you with dates and time very soon.

Sincerely., Janice Winter, Recreation Dept.

The next few weeks Deb and I were busy with all the activities relating to "Mom's Trip", reservations, shopping, dovetailing everything into our schedules. What is the weather in Detroit in June? What shall I wear.? What should I take besides the old cribbage board?

I wrote to Miss Winter with my schedule and all the pieces were falling into place.

Soon it was June and I was in the car on the way to the airport getting more and more nervous as each mile passed by. I almost told Deb to turn around and go back a couple of times but I stuck to my convictions that I would go, and I wanted to go. As I waved good-bye to the Jacksonville skyline, I knew Detroit would be so much different, bigger and older and foreign to me. What the heck, it was time for me to have a new adventure.

Deb seemed to be as excited as I was as we hugged and parted at the gate. I hadn't traveled alone for quite some time so I knew I had to really take charge and do everything right and not get lost or get in the wrong line. or on the wrong plane.

We were soon airborne and having a window seat I was able to enjoy the Jacksonville skyline and try to pick out landmarks. Soon we were up in the clouds and with no seatmate to divert my attention, I had nothing to occupy me but my thoughts of things to come, but my thoughts drifted to the past, and I was trying to remember exactly how Roy and I met. However, I drew a blank. How could I not remember how we met?

I remember very clearly how I met Leonard. in June of 1949. I was working on a private case at Tompkins County Hospital with a Mr. S. who had a very bad temper who really didn't need a special nurse. He needed a gofer. He had me go downtown to Myers Smoke Shop to get him the Wall Street Journal. Another time he had me go to the north end of Ithaca to his house to pick up his clean laundry, but mostly he had me read the Bible to him. He never got mad at me but he did get angry at a visitor to another patient in the room and threw his grape juice at the lady who insisted that he pay to have her clothes dry cleaned.

A friend of mine, a staff nurse in the same floor told me she had someone she wanted me to meet. So she took me into a nearby room to meet Leonard, who was a patient there as the Cornell Infirmary was closed in the summer. Leonard was a teaching fellow at Cornell in the division of modern languages studying for his Ph D. He was not too ill but had just been diagnosed with Hodgkins Disease (pseudo leukemia). We became friends and when I was off duty I had occasion to take him out for a ride along the east coast of the lake in my Chevy as a special outing for him.

He was soon discharged from the hospital and went back to his fraternity , Zeta Beta Tau. We had a fine summer seeing each other often while I worked and he studied until one night I'll never forget. I was on the night shift and talking with one of the other nurses and the subject of Leonard came up and this nurse told me he had given her a framed painting, oil on silk of a flower. He had given me the same thing, an oil on silk of an orchid. (I still have it on the wall of my family room). I was so furious or jealous or hurt, whatever, that as soon as I got off duty at 7 AM, I drove up to the campus, entered the fraternity house, stormed up the stairs to find him and woke him up and told him what happened and asked him to explain. Somehow he calmed me down and we went out for breakfast. And I was reassured all was well between us and we continued to date throughout the summer.

Some time later that summer I received in the mail a giant "greeting card" about 18 x 14 inches with pictures he had drawn and the following verse:

> A damsel with honey—colored hair,
> In a vision once I saw
> 'Twas a Delmar Denman
> And a jewel of rare degree
> Upon my heartstrings she played
> A magic hit parade.
> Singing of enchanting joys.
> Could I revive within me

Her symphony and song
To such a deep delight 'twould win me
That with music loud and long
And all who heard should see them there
I would build a golden dome in air

A sunny dome with caves of ice
And all should cry, Beware! Beware!
His flashing eyes, his floating hair!
Weave a circle round him thrice
And close your eyes with holy dread
For he on honey-dew hath fed,
And drunk the milk of Paradise

I was pretty thrilled at receiving this big card and the special verse. It wasn't until years later that I was watching a movie in which the suitor was reading to his girl from "Kubla Kahn" by Samuel Taylor Coleridge. My verse from Leonard was a parody of that. I should have known since he was an English Major and I had studied only medicine. I was just happy that he really cared about me. He was so smart and so very special.

By the end of summer he hadn't returned to good health and flew down to Long Island to Burke's Institute for rehab., shortly thereafter he was transferred to Memorial Hospital , Sloan Kettering Cancer Hospital in New York City.

I followed him down there and rented a room at Barbizon Hotel for Women and got a job at New York Hospital, Cornell Medical Canter, where I had studied medicine and pediatrics, in 1942. almost directly across the street from Memorial. I worked nights and spent time during the day with him and sometimes slept. I moved out of Barbizon to a room in a 6 floor walk up near the hospitals.

We made good friends with the volunteer, Donald Hurst and the family of the other patient in the room whose names I can't recall.

I draw a real blank with some names, and some places. This lovely couple let me stay in their apartment and with their help and that of Mr Hurst, Leonard and I were married in a simple ceremony at their home as soon as he was discharged from the hospital. We went directly to Hotel Standish Hall (I think that was the name) where I had obtained an apartment and we set up housekeeping. But his condition didn't improve so I had him admitted to Flower Fifth Ave. Hospital, the only hospital with an empty bed. The doctor gave me carte blanc to order anything I wanted for him. In due time he was well enough to be discharged and we went directly to the airport and flew to Bermuda to get some R and R. Our room was on the second floor with no elevator and stairs too difficult for Leonard to navigate. Also as it was rainy and cold, we flew over to Nassau for a better situation.

Despite the tincture of time and warm weather Leonard wasn't getting much stronger so we headed back to the states for good medical care. We rented a small one bedroom cottage in. Ft.Lauderdale and he would go to Broward General Hospital for blood transfusions every few days. We would go for daily walks near our cottage but he still couldn't get back his strength and we soon took a train back to New York City where he could see his doctor, Dr. Craven. We went by ambulance to New York Hospital and they had no bed, but finally Memorial Hospital said they had a Damon Runyon bed where they would admit him. I well remember overhearing some of the interns laughing that we had gotten married. It wasn't the first time I had been asked why I would marry him. He had Hodgkin's Disease ! Should I just leave him because he had that disease? Dr. Craver said his case was non aggressive but that didn't prove to be true. In any case he wasn't a person I would desert for any reason. And I didn't. I was with him a few days later when he died.

When we returned from Florida and he was admitted to the hospital , I was able to rent again that 6th floor walk-up near the hospital. Leonard had signed a document to donate his eyes after death and the enucleation had to be done very soon after death. So I had to rush back to the rented room and run up the six flights of stairs and hunt for the document in our luggage.

Upon finding it I rushed back to the hospital to give it to the right authority. Later someone from Riverside Chapel came over for some clothes, but didn't need the shoes. What did I know about those things?

I have never been able to remove from my memory the nightmare I had. soon thereafter. I dreamed he hadn't really died, I was in the hospital room with him and he wanted me to help him open his eyes so he could see me. I suppose that kind of dream or similar ones happen when one loses a loved one. I said my final good bye at the chapel and soon went back home to my parents in Ithaca.

Since my car was still in Florida,(I had hired someone to drive it to Florida from upstate New York so we would have the use of it in Ft. Lauderdale) and I needed it for work. I returned to Ft. Lauderdale by train and went back to work at Broward General Hospital. One day I found a ticket stuffed under my windshield wiper at work. It was a police citation for working in Florida with an out of state tag. I went to the police station and told them I was returning north in a few weeks. They were very insistent. I had to get a Florida registration. if I wanted to continue to work here. So I got my beautiful Florida tag and continued to work for several weeks on a case I had already started.

I was staying in a house my cousin Don had built and had not yet sold. I bought a used refrigerator and a few odds and ends of furniture, just enough for a few weeks. Some time later I got a wild hair and wrote to my mother and asked if she would like to come down to Ft. Lauderdale and stay a few days and accompany me back home. She hadn't visited Florida for many years, not since before she was married, so she agreed without hesitation. I sent her train fare and soon I was picking her up at the station in Ft. Lauderdale. My few furnishings sufficed for "camping out" for a short while for the two of us. Soon after her arrival cousin Jack was in town and we invited him to bunk with us. He had a sleeping bag and pillow with a pillow case heavily embroidered that his mom had packed for him. He was single but getting ready to get married. The three of us spent a few days together and he showed us areas of interest that he was familiar with, i. e. Hialeah Race track, with all the pink flamingoes in the center, Univ of Miami, etc. After he left, my mom and I went to Key West for a few days before packing up and heading back to Ithaca.

We enjoyed the trip back to Ithaca with several stops along the way, Marineland, McKee Jungle Gardens, and a stopover in New York City to see a Broadway show in which Eva Gabor appeared. Ralph Ballamy was in the audience and waved to everyone as he walked up the aisle.

My mom and I always enjoyed doing things together just as my daughter and I do today. One day after we returned to Ithaca, we decided to go downtown to see a real trial in progress. Part way through the case we were paged to come to the phone. Dad had fallen off the roof and fractured his pelvis. He later told me that when hit the ground his hat had blown off and he crawled along the ground to retrieve his hat, thinking all would be well if he had his hat on! Then he crawled into the house and called an ambulance. We were scared and pretty worried, not knowing the extent of his injuries or his general condition. We immediately left the court house and rushed to the hospital. After an overly long interrogation at the admitting office we were finally directed to the area where dad was on a stretcher acting normal and not uncomfortable. Mom was additionally concerned because she had left the dishes in the sink that morning as we' d had to leave early for the courthouse. She never leaves the dishes undone or the beds unmade.

We are all very close in our family and I remember that was the one thing that Leonard admired about us. His family had been quite different. Once back in Ithaca from Florida, I had to get back to work again, doing private duty until I could find a steady job.

*　　*　　*

Up here in the clouds it is easy to day dream and hard to know where you are with no signs or buildings or other landmarks for guidance. The only clue is by your watch and figure where you are in flight time. With still no activity nearby to distract me and no desire to read I am free to let my mind wander and it will. At home there is always plenty to do, in the house and in the yard but away from home it is different. I am used to keeping busy with the only time to squander in day dreams is in the middle of the night trying to get back to sleep. And I surely don't want to remember things that anger me, and there are plenty. Unpleasant thoughts rule out any chance to return to sleep.

PAULINE D. WEBB, (LT. PAULINE A. DENMAN, A. N. C. WWII)

I also remember how I met Cecil. Someone wanted us to meet. Maybe that is how it should be, i. e. someone who knows both parties and thinks it would be a good match. Maybe that is how I met Roy, why can't I remember? I vaguely recall being out with a group (always a group on Tinian) and seeing Roy with a girl named Wendy. Sometime later, after we had been dating, Roy and I would joke about "wendy" curtains when we saw wind blowing curtains in the windows. But I have no memory of going from point A to point B, seeing each other and dating.

Back in Ithaca I was on a private case in a home caring for the mother of two high profile Ithaca attorneys. I was warned in advance by the nursing agency that she was the mother of these attorneys and some nurses had refused the case, I was new in town and knew nothing about the family and I rarely refused cases even though other nurses had done so. I somehow always got along with people and would form new friendships with the families.

One of her sons, Charlie a pre med student at Cornell lived at home. We became friends, I drove him to school occasionally and we dated a bit, went dancing. I also became friends with one of the daughters, Sarah, who lived at home and cared for her mother in the day time, (I was on the night shift). We sometimes went out for lunch or a soda.

Charlie had been engaged to Joyce Webb who was studying art at Pratt Institute in Brooklyn. When she was home from school she worked in the local pharmacy where I did a lot of business. Ithaca is a small town and everyone knows too much about everyone. Joyce must have known I was dating Charlie because the pharmacist told me that Joyce wished I would get, "On a Slow Boat to China". To make matters worse, Charlie decided to play a joke (?) on Joyce. He drove my car and we went by the campsite at Lower Enfield Falls where Joyce and her dad were camping for a week. We just drove by and waved. Just youthful foolishness.

It was much later, in the winter when Charlie said he wanted me to meet someone. It was Joyce's recently divorced father, Cecil. I was amenable to his suggestion. To set up the meeting, Charlie had Cecil hold a party at his apartment so that we could meet. It was a nice party, some couples and some singles. Two of the singles asked me for dates, but Cecil is the one I chose. I recall being apprehensive about telling my parents I was dating Joyce's father! But they liked him and I remember he sent my mom a dozen roses on Valentine's Day. I doubt she had ever had a bouquet of roses. I don't remember what he gave me but he sure thrilled my mom. Cecil and I were twelve years apart in age but close in interests, and that is what really counts. About six months later he and I went to the wedding of Sarah's sister Josephine and it made Cecil think we should get married, and a few months later we did. It was a good marriage producing two wonderful children. It ended suddenly at our home in Florida when he had a fatal heart attack. Our children were age fourteen and ten and it was a terrible blow to all of us.

I don't want to think about the trials and tribulations that followed his death. I want to think about today and tomorrow, not yesterday, and wonder how things will turn out. I soon will know when we come out of the clouds.

The flight was uneventful (thank goodness) and Detroit was just ahead (below). I am sure my driver will be there as scheduled. Not to worry.

After deplaning and collecting my luggage I went out to the concourse to look for my driver. There were several men and women holding big signs over their heads with a person's last name on them. It didn't take long to see WEBB in big bold letters so I knew my ride was there.

I was so revved up in anticipation of seeing Roy that I hardly absorbed the streets of Detroit. When the driver said we had arrived , I was able to see the beautifully landscaped entry to Detroit Senior Village. Such a lovely setting of many single family homes, larger buildings of perhaps townhouses, flowerbeds, shade trees, everything in springtime glory.

The driver escorted me into the lobby of the recreation building where Miss Winter was there to meet me. She was as lovely and gracious as her letters had indicated. We introduced ourselves and she told me that Roy was there in the lounge reading the daily paper. totally unaware of what was soon to happen.

I deposited my luggage at the desk and handed her the old Cribbage board and asked her to go and hand it to Roy and say she had found someone to play Cribbage with him.

When he saw the Cribbage board and scrutinized it, he dropped his newspaper on the floor and hopped out of his chair.

"Where did you find this? It has my initials on it"

Miss Winter pointed to me standing in the door way. He immediately headed my way.

As he walked toward me, all the years melted away and I was back in our Quonset recreation room on Tinian. There he was with that special grin and light in his eye, his Cribbage board in one hand and his beat up old seventeen mission hat in the other, ready for another game of Cribbage and a glass of lemonade.

Today he looked much the same as he approached me, "Pill, Pill, is it really you? You came to see ME?". With tears in my eyes I replied, "Yes, yes" whereupon he grabbed me and hugged me and took my breath away. The best bear hug ever. Neither one of us could break away.

Whoever said, "It only happens in the movies" was all wrong. We were together again.

PART III

THE REST OF THE STORY

He held me so tight, so warm and right. Just like I remember from that long ago "good bye" on Tinian. This time I wouldn't, I couldn't let go. After all these years I was again all wrapped up in his arms.

When I finally did pull away I felt entangled, entrapped, not in his arms, but in the sheets on my bed at home in Jacksonville. I couldn't get untangled, I didn't want to break that final thread. I had found him at last and no going back to Jacksonville. How could it be a dream! How could that be? It was all so real, so logical, no way it could be just a dream. Dreams are illogical, frustrating and short. This was too real, too logical. Let me go back to sleep and be back with him and finish the dream.

The only thing a bit off the reality of true life was the SNAFU from the army in reporting the death. They don't make those kind of mistakes. Just wishful thinking on my part. I suppose. I should have realized that kind of mistake wouldn't happen.

Lots of dreams are nightmares or distressing enough to wake me up, but this was so perfect it has to be true. Maybe I will come to and be back in Detroit.

I am willing to accept the fact that I am back home and Detroit was just a dream. But what a beautiful dream.

My current life here in Jacksonville is very enjoyable and I am content but I had such high hopes. That knock on the door could have brought a new chapter into my life. I have plenty of time as I plan to live to be one hundred and that is a long way off as I am not even ninety yet. There is still time for new chapters. And I wanted Roy to be in those chapters, like none of the others from all those days of long ago.

I am not only content but very thankful to still be able to drive my car and ride my bike and look after my house. I finally gave up mowing the lawn when the lawn mower rusted out and I now have a man who keeps it mowed and trimmed much better that I could. I used to get on the extension ladder and climb on the roof to clean out the gutters, but Deb put her foot down and took the ladder to her house. I still have and use my five foot step ladder where needed.

I appreciate the fact that I am healthy. Must be the whole wheat bread and tablespoons of cod liver oil that dad insisted on in addition to always playing outdoors, and never being allowed to eat the Halloween candy until after supper each night , one piece only!

Whatever the reason, I count my blessings every day for all that I have and especially my devoted children who keep in touch constantly. What more could I possibly wish for? Maybe a few more beautiful dreams. There was a pretty song many years ago titled, "I Can Dream Can't I". I don't recall the lyrics, but they might apply. Who knows?

"When you arise in the morning, think of what a precious privilege it is to be alive – to breathe, to think, to enjoy, to love." Marcus Aurelius, Roman emperor and philosopher.

THE END

CPSIA information can be obtained at www.ICGtesting.com
Printed in the USA
LVOW080126120512

281406LV00001B/10/P